FARMHOUSE
COOKING

FARMHOUSE COOKING

the best of country home cooking with
200 fresh and seasonal recipes shown
step-by-step in over 700 photographs

EDITOR LIZ TRIGG

southwater

This edition is published by Southwater

Southwater is an imprint of Anness Publishing Ltd

Hermes House, 88–89 Blackfriars Road, London SE1 8HA

tel. 020 7401 2077; fax 020 7633 9499

www.southwaterbooks.com; info@anness.com

© Anness Publishing Ltd 1997, 2005

UK agent: The Manning Partnership Ltd, 6 The Old Dairy, Melcombe Road, Bath BA2 3L
tel. 01225 478444; fax 01225 478440; sales@manning-partnership.co.uk

UK distributor: Grantham Book Services Ltd, Isaac Newton Way, Alma Park Industrial Estate
Grantham, Lincs NG31 9SD; tel. 01476 541080; fax 01476 541061; orders@gbs.tbs-ltd.co.uk

North American agent/distributor: National Book Network, 4501 Forbes Boulevard, Suite 200
Lanham, MD 20706; tel. 301 459 3366; fax 301 429 5746; www.nbnbooks.com

Australian agent/distributor: Pan Macmillan Australia, Level 18, St Martins Tower,
31 Market St, Sydney, NSW 2000; tel. 1300 135 113; fax 1300 135 103
customer.service@macmillan.com.au

New Zealand agent/distributor: David Bateman Ltd, 30 Tarndale Grove, Off Bush Road, Albany, Auckland
tel. (09) 415 7664; fax (09) 415 8892

Publisher: Joanna Lorenz
Project Editor: Gaby Goldsack
Editor: Jenni Fleetwood
Designer: Siân Keogh, Axis Design
Illustrator: Anna Koska

The publishers would like to thank the following contributors:
Carla Capalbo, Jacqueline Clark, Maxine Clark Cleary, Carole Clements, Stephanie Donaldson,
Joanna Farrow, Christine France, Christine Ingram,
Judy Jackson, Patricia Lousada, Norma MacMillan, Katherine Richmond,
Laura Washburn, Steven Wheeler, Elizabeth Wolf-Cohen.

They would also like to thank the following photographers:
Karl Adamson, Edward Allwright, James Duncan, John Freeman, Michelle Garrett,
Amanda Heywood, Patrick McLeavey.

Previously published as *The Farmhouse Cookbook*

1 3 5 7 9 10 8 6 4 2

Contents

Introduction

The essence of farmhouse cooking is not dependent on geography; it can be enjoyed whether you live in a country cottage or urban town house. This book is full of mouth watering recipes that can be enjoyed in any locality. Throughout the emphasis is on fresh country foods that provide wholesome country fare. Whether you are out to impress special guests or simply want to create a wholesome meal to fill your family after a long, hard day, the recipes in this book will give you plenty of rustic meals to choose from.

Farmhouse Cookery

Some of the finest cooking in the world is to be found in farmhouses. Whether these are sited alongside English orchards, among French vineyards, on the Canadian prairie or in the green hills of New Zealand, one factor will be constant – the kitchen will be the heart of the homestead.

A love of good food is common to all country folk. Working the land is one of the finest ways of stimulating the appetite, and what better way to satisfy hunger than to enjoy a fine meal, flavoured with freshly picked herbs and served with fresh vegetables straight from the kitchen garden?

It is this availability of first class raw materials that has given farmhouse cooking its essential character: by and large it is simple, satisfying food with few frills. When you can wander between rows of salad stuff, lifting a lettuce here, a bunch of radishes there, then pausing to pick a few young sorrel leaves and some chives, your salad will not need an elaborate dressing. When pick-your-own means literally that, and you can combine your very own strawberries with cream from cows you know by name, you have the means of making a dessert no restaurant could better.

Of course, there are some drawbacks. Unlike the town dweller who can pop into a supermarket for produce from all around the world all through the year, the farmhouse cook tends to use whatever he or she has to hand. Perhaps that is no bad thing. Many of us have forgotten the pleasure in podding the first peas or digging up early potatoes so tiny and tasty that it seems sacrilege even to add butter to them. When asparagus is not something you can have whenever you want, but is a rare treat in a short season, it becomes all the more special.

Farmhouse cooks step beyond their own gardens and get to know the riches of the countryside, too. They gather mushrooms and hazelnuts, know where there are still sloe bushes to be found, and pick wild blackberries for making into pies, cobblers and charlottes.

The farming year is punctuated with festivals. Easter is marked with special breads and cakes; centrepiece for the harvest thanksgiving is a loaf in the shape of a wheatsheaf; and the coming of Christmas is an excuse for a positive orgy of baking, as mincemeat, puddings and cakes are prepared, along with pickles and chutneys to serve on Boxing Day.

Farmhouse cooks like nothing more than a celebration, and are never happier than when cooking for a crowd. Depending on the country – and the season – dining rooms will be dusted or tables taken into the garden, flowers will be picked, wine mulled or chilled, and enough food cooked to feed a small army. And if extra guests arrive unexpectedly, so much the better – after all, there'll be plenty of food to go round.

That food is celebrated in this book. You'll find pâtés, pies and puddings within its pages, alongside substantial stews and simple salads. Some of the dishes are slow-cooked for melting tenderness; others are swift solutions to those occasions when there's little time for complicated cooking – and all are utterly delicious!

LEFT: *The harvest loaf is a potent symbol of country life.*
OPPOSITE: *The farmhouse cook relies upon fresh seasonal produce.*

The Farmhouse Kitchen Garden

If the kitchen is the heart of the farmhouse, the kitchen garden is what supplies its strength. Having fresh herbs and vegetables within easy reach makes all the difference to country cooking. A *bouquet garni* that consists of fresh parsley, thyme and bay gives so much more flavour than something that resembles a tea bag, and gathering the herbs from your own plants is supremely satisfying.

Of course, you don't have to live in a farmhouse to reap the benefits of your own kitchen garden. A small sunny plot near the kitchen door is ideal, but you can garden in tubs or even pots on the windowsill.

Growing your own herbs gives you a wonderful opportunity to experiment with some of the more unusual varieties. Specialist herb growers have a wide range of young plants in pots, and are usually so enthusiastic about their produce that they will not only give growing tips, but will also share favourite recipes. Seed catalogues are a good source of supply, too, and a good way of involving younger members of the family. Children enjoy choosing and planting their own seeds, and are far less likely to be fussy about trying dishes flavoured with herbs when they have grown them themselves. The same goes for vegetables – involve children in the cultivation and the cooking (and eating) will come naturally.

PLANTING SEEDS
Every packet of seeds carries instructions for planting. If you are growing herbs and salad leaves for the windowsill, you can germinate seeds in partitioned trays and transfer the plants, as they grow, to well-drained pots until they are large enough to be planted in the garden. Regular watering and plenty of sun will ensure an abundance of freshness and flavour.

Tomatoes can be grown from seed, but many gardeners prefer to buy young plants. Tomato plants do well in growing bags on a patio and are best positioned against a south-facing wall. Vegetables such as carrots, radishes, beetroot and turnips are best planted in rich soil in an open bed. Seedlings that grow too close together should be thinned to enable proper development. Young thinnings are delicious in fresh colourful salads.

GROWING IN POTS
Salad leaves and herbs can be grown successfully in terracotta pots. Regular watering is important, but you should check the seed packet or a gardening book to determine how much. Some herbs love water, but many Mediterranean plants prefer it if the soil is left until it is almost dry before being given a thorough soaking. All pots should allow for drainage.

For a constant supply of lettuce, sow seeds at fortnightly intervals throughout the summer and pick when needed (many new varieties allow you to take only as many leaves as you require, while the plant continues to grow). In colder weather, herbs and salad leaves should be kept under glass to maximize warmth from the sun. Many herbs enjoy a sunny spot on an inside window ledge.

PICKING AND STORING HERBS
Ideally, herbs should be used as soon as they are picked. If this is not possible, store them with care. In season, bunches of parsley, mint, coriander and chives keep well in jugs of water in the fridge. Cover the top of each jug with a plastic bag. Thyme, rosemary, lavender and bay leaves can be tied in bunches and hung in a well-ventilated cupboard to dry. Dried herbs will keep for several months.

French Dressing with Herbs

A herb dressing makes the perfect partner for a simple green salad.

INGREDIENTS

60 ml / 4 tbsp extra virgin olive oil
30 ml / 2 tbsp groundnut or sunflower oil
15 ml / 1 tbsp lemon juice
60 ml / 4 tbsp finely chopped fresh herbs, such as parsley, chives, tarragon and marjoram
pinch of caster sugar

Makes about 120 ml / 4 fl oz / ½ cup

1

Place the olive and groundnut or sunflower oil in a screw-top jar.

2

Add the lemon juice, herbs and sugar. Screw on the lid and shake well.

TOP LEFT AND ABOVE: *Grow seeds in small trays on the windowsill, then transplant to individual pots. When large enough, plant them in the garden.*

TOP RIGHT: *Store chives and flat-leaf parsley in a water-filled jar in the fridge. Lavender and thyme can be tied in bunches and dried.*

Making Meat Stock

As every farmhouse cook will tell you, good home-made stock is the secret of successful meat soups, stews, casseroles, gravies and sauces.

INGREDIENTS

1.75 kg / 4–4½ lb beef bones, such as shin, leg, neck and clod, or veal or lamb bones, cut in 6 cm / 2½ in pieces
2 onions, unpeeled, quartered
2 carrots, roughly chopped
2 celery sticks, with leaves if possible, roughly chopped
2 tomatoes, coarsely chopped

4 litres / 6½ pints / 16 cups water
a handful of parsley stalks
a few fresh thyme sprigs or ¾ teaspoon dried thyme
2 bay leaves
10 black peppercorns, lightly crushed

Makes about 2 litres / 3½ pints/ 18 cups

1

Preheat the oven to 230°C / 450°F / Gas Mark 8. Put the bones in a roasting tin or flameproof casserole and roast, turning occasionally, for 30 minutes or until they start to brown.

2

Add the vegetables and baste with the fat in the tin or casserole. Roast for a further 20–30 minutes or until the bones are well browned. Stir and baste occasionally.

3

Transfer the bones and vegetables to a stockpot. Spoon off the fat from the roasting tin or casserole, add a little water and bring to the boil, scraping in any residue. Pour this liquid into the stockpot.

4

Add the remaining water. Bring just to the boil, skimming frequently to remove any foam. Add the herbs and peppercorns.

5

Partly cover the pot and simmer the stock for 4–6 hours, topping up the liquid as necessary.

6

Strain the stock. Skim as much fat as possible from the surface. If possible, cool the stock and then chill it; the fat will set in a layer on the surface and can be removed easily.

Making Chicken Stock

Use turkey to make the stock, if you prefer.

INGREDIENTS

*1.2–1.4 kg / 2½–3 lb chicken wings,
backs and necks (chicken, turkey, etc)
2 onions, unpeeled, quartered
4 litres / 6½ pints / 16 cups water
2 carrots, roughly chopped
2 celery sticks, with leaves if possible,
roughly chopped
a small handful of fresh parsley
a few fresh thyme sprigs or ¾ teaspoon
dried thyme
1 or 2 bay leaves
10 black peppercorns, lightly crushed*

Makes about 2.5 litres / 4 pints / 10 cups

1

Put the chicken pieces and the onions in a
stockpot. Cook over a medium heat,
stirring occasionally, until lightly browned.
Stir in the water. Bring to the boil. Skim
the surface.

2

Add the remaining ingredients. Simmer for
3 hours. Strain, cool and chill. When cold,
remove the fat from the surface.

Making Vegetable Stock

Vary the ingredients for this fresh-flavoured stock according to what you have to hand.

INGREDIENTS

*2 large onions, coarsely chopped
2 leeks, sliced
3 garlic cloves, crushed
3 carrots, coarsely chopped
4 celery sticks, coarsely chopped
1 large strip of pared lemon rind
a handful of parsley stalks
a few fresh thyme sprigs
2 bay leaves
2.5 litres / 4 pints / 10 cups water*

Makes 2.5 litres / 4 pints / 10 cups

1

Put the vegetables, lemon rind, herbs and
water in a stockpot and bring to the boil.
Skim the surface.

2

Reduce the heat and simmer, uncovered, for
30 minutes. Strain the stock and leave it
to cool.

Soups
and Starters

In the farmhouse kitchen, stock simmers on the stove, ready to form the basis of a nourishing soup to satisfy appetites honed by hard work and an early start. When the harvest is in, there'll be time for more leisurely meals, prefaced by pâtés, patties and simple salads. The following selection of delicious soups and starters have been selected from farmhouse kitchens around the world. There are recipes to suit all occasions and tastes.

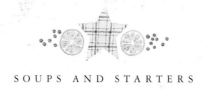
Country Vegetable Soup

This satisfying soup captures all the flavours of the countryside. The basil and garlic purée gives it extra colour and a wonderful aroma — so don't omit it.

INGREDIENTS

275 g / 10 oz / 1½ cups fresh shelled broad beans, or 175 g / 6 oz / ¾ cup dried haricot beans, soaked overnight in water to cover
2.5 ml / ½ tsp dried herbes de Provence
2 garlic cloves, finely chopped
15 ml / 1 tbsp olive oil
1 onion, finely chopped
2 small leeks, finely sliced
1 celery stick, finely sliced
2 carrots, finely diced
2 small potatoes, peeled and finely diced
115 g / 4 oz French beans
1.2 litres / 2 pints / 5 cups water
115 g / 4 oz / 1 cup peas, fresh or frozen
2 small courgettes, finely chopped
3 tomatoes, skinned, seeded and finely chopped
a handful of spinach leaves, cut into thin ribbons
salt and freshly ground black pepper
fresh basil sprigs, to garnish

For the garlic purée
1 or 2 garlic cloves, finely chopped
15 g / ½ oz / ½ cup basil leaves
60 ml / 4 tbsp grated Parmesan cheese
60 ml / 4 tbsp extra virgin olive oil

Serves 6–8

NOTE
To serve the soup, season and swirl a spoonful of purée into each bowl and garnish with basil.

1

To make the purée, process the garlic, basil and Parmesan until smooth. With the machine running, slowly add the olive oil through the feed-tube. Alternatively, put the garlic, basil and cheese in a mortar. Pound with a pestle, then stir in the oil.

2

If using dried beans, boil vigorously for 10 minutes and drain. Place them or fresh beans in a saucepan with the herbs and 1 garlic clove. Add water to cover by 2.5 cm / 1 in. Bring to the boil and simmer for 10 minutes for fresh beans or about 1 hour for dried beans.

3

Heat the oil in a saucepan. Fry the onion and leeks for 5 minutes, stirring occasionally.

4

Add the celery and carrots, with the remaining garlic clove. Cook for 10 minutes.

5

Add the potatoes, French beans and water. Bring to the boil, then cover and simmer for 10 minutes.

6

Add the peas, courgettes and tomatoes, with the reserved beans. Simmer for 25–30 minutes. Add the spinach, season to taste, and simmer for 5 minutes.

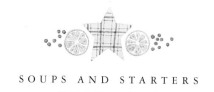

Herb and Chilli Gazpacho

Gazpacho is a lovely soup, set off perfectly by the addition of a few herbs.

INGREDIENTS

1.2 kg / 2½ lb ripe tomatoes
225 g / 8 oz onions
2 green peppers
1 green chilli
1 large cucumber
30 ml / 2 tbsp red wine vinegar
15 ml / 1 tbsp balsamic vinegar
30 ml / 2 tbsp olive oil
1 clove of garlic, peeled and crushed
300 ml / ½ pint tomato juice
30 ml / 2 tbsp tomato purée
salt and pepper
2 tbsp finely chopped mixed fresh herbs, plus some extra to garnish

Serves 6

1

Keep back about a quarter of all the fresh vegetables, except the green chilli, and place all the remaining ingredients in a food processor and season to taste. Process finely and chill in the refrigerator.

2

Chop all the remaining vegetables and serve in a separate bowl to sprinkle over the soup. Crush some ice cubes and add to the centre of each bowl and garnish with fresh herbs. Serve with bread rolls.

Pear and Watercress Soup with Stilton Croûtons

Pears and Stilton taste very good when you eat them together after the main course –
here, for a change, they are served as a starter.

INGREDIENTS

1 bunch watercress
4 medium pears, sliced
900 ml / 1½ pints chicken stock,
preferably home-made
salt and pepper
120 ml / 4 fl oz double cream
juice of 1 lime

For the croûtons
25 g / 1 oz butter
30 ml / 1 tbsp olive oil
200 g / 7 oz cubed stale bread
140 g / 5 oz chopped Stilton cheese

Serves 6

1

Keep back about a third of the watercress
leaves. Place all the rest of the watercress
leaves and stalks in a pan with the pears,
stock and a little seasoning. Simmer for
about 15–20 minutes.

2

Reserving some watercress leaves for
garnishing, add the rest of the leaves and
immediately blend in a food processor until
smooth.

3

Put the mixture into a bowl and stir in the
cream and lime juice to mix the flavours
thoroughly. Season again to taste. Pour all
the soup back into a pan and reheat,
stirring gently until warmed through.

4

To make the croûtons, melt the butter and
oil and fry the bread cubes until golden
brown. Drain on kitchen paper. Put the
cheese on top and heat under a hot grill
until bubbling. Reheat the soup and pour
into bowls. Divide the croûtons and
remaining watercress between the bowls.

Green Bean Soup with Parmesan

Make the most of a garden glut of green beans by serving this colourful summer soup.

INGREDIENTS

25 g / 1 oz / 2 tbsp butter
225 g / 8 oz green beans, trimmed
1 garlic clove, crushed
475 ml / 16 fl oz / 2 cups vegetable
stock
50 g / 2 oz / ⅔ cup Parmesan cheese
60 ml / 4 tbsp single cream
30 ml / 2 tbsp chopped fresh parsley
salt and freshly ground black pepper

Serves 4

1

Melt the butter in a saucepan and cook the
green beans and garlic for 2–3 minutes over
a medium heat, stirring frequently. Stir in
the stock with salt and pepper to taste.
Bring to the boil. Reduce the heat and
simmer for 10–15 minutes, until the beans
are tender.

2

Process the soup until smooth.
Alternatively, purée the soup in a food mill.
Return it to the clean pan and heat gently.
Stir in the Parmesan and cream. Sprinkle
with the parsley and serve.

Lentil and Vegetable Soup

*Unlike red lentils, the brown variety retain their shape after cooking
and add texture to this hearty country soup.*

INGREDIENTS

175 g / 6 oz / 1 cup brown lentils
1 litre / 1¾ pints / 4 cups chicken
stock
250 ml / 8 fl oz / 1 cup water
60 ml / 4 tbsp dry red wine
675 g / 1½ lb tomatoes, skinned,
seeded and chopped, or 400 g / 14 oz
canned chopped tomatoes
1 carrot, sliced
1 onion, chopped
1 celery stick, sliced
1 garlic clove, crushed
¼ tsp ground coriander
10 ml / 2 tsp snipped fresh basil, or
½ tsp dried basil
1 bay leaf
90 ml / 6 tbsp freshly grated
Parmesan cheese

Serves 6

1

Put the lentils in a sieve. Rinse under cold
running water, then discard any discoloured
ones and any grit.

3

Reduce the heat to low, cover and simmer
for 20–25 minutes, stirring occasionally.
When the lentils are tender, discard the bay
leaf and ladle the soup into 6 warmed
bowls. Sprinkle each portion with 15 ml /
1 tbsp of the Parmesan.

2

Put the lentils in a large saucepan. Add all
the remaining ingredients, except the
Parmesan, and bring to the boil.

NOTE

For a more substantial soup, add about
115 g / 4 oz / ½ cup finely chopped cooked
ham for the last 10 minutes of cooking.

Borscht

This rustic soup was the staple diet of pre-revolutionary Russian peasants for centuries.
There are many variations and it is rare to find two recipes the same.

INGREDIENTS

350 g / 12 oz whole, uncooked beetroot
15 ml / 1 tbsp sunflower oil
115 g / 4 oz rindless streaky bacon rashers, chopped
1 large onion, chopped
1 large carrot, cut into matchstick strips
3 celery sticks, thinly sliced
1.5 litres / 2½ pints / 6 cups chicken stock
about 225 g / 8 oz tomatoes, skinned, seeded and sliced
about 30 ml / 2 tbsp lemon juice or wine vinegar
30 ml / 2 tbsp chopped fresh dill
115 g / 4 oz white cabbage, thinly sliced
150 ml / ¼ pint / ⅔ cup soured cream
salt and freshly ground black pepper

Serves 6

1

Peel the beetroot, slice and then cut into very thin strips. Heat the oil in a large, heavy-based saucepan and fry the bacon over a gentle heat for 3–4 minutes.

2

Add the onion to the pan, fry for 2–3 minutes and then add the carrot, celery and beetroot. Cook for 4–5 minutes, stirring frequently, until the oil has been absorbed.

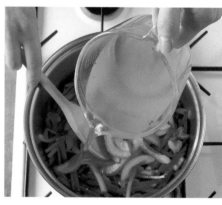

3

Add the stock, tomatoes, lemon juice or wine vinegar and half of the dill. Season, then bring to the boil, lower the heat and simmer for about 30–40 minutes until the vegetables are completely tender.

4

Add the cabbage and simmer for 5 minutes until tender. Adjust the seasoning and serve, swirled with the soured cream and sprinkled with the remaining dill.

Farmhouse Onion Soup

Slow, careful cooking is the secret of this traditional onion soup.

INGREDIENTS

*30 ml / 2 tbsp sunflower or olive oil,
or a mixture
25 g / 1 oz / 2 tbsp butter
4 large onions, chopped
900 ml / 1½ pints / 3¾ cups beef stock
4 slices French bread
40–50 g / 1½–2 oz Gruyère or
Cheddar cheese, grated
salt and freshly ground black pepper*

Serves 4

1

Heat the oil and butter in a deep saucepan and fry the onions briskly for 3–4 minutes. Reduce the heat and cook gently for 45–60 minutes.

2

When the onions are a rich mahogany brown, add the beef stock and a little seasoning. Simmer, partially covered, for 30 minutes, then taste and adjust the seasoning.

3

Preheat the grill and toast the French bread. Spoon the soup into four soup dishes that can safely be used under the grill. Place a piece of bread in each. Sprinkle with the cheese and grill for a few minutes until golden.

Summer Tomato Soup

The success of this soup depends on using ripe, full-flavoured tomatoes, such as the oval plum variety. It is traditionally made when the tomato season is at its peak.

INGREDIENTS

15 ml / 1 tbsp olive oil
1 large onion, chopped
1 carrot, chopped
1 kg / 2¼ lb ripe tomatoes, cored and quartered
2 garlic cloves, chopped
5 fresh thyme sprigs
4 or 5 fresh marjoram sprigs, plus extra for garnish
1 bay leaf
45 ml / 3 tbsp soured cream or yogurt, plus a little extra to garnish
salt and freshly ground black pepper

Serves 4

1

Heat the olive oil in a large saucepan. Cook the onion and carrot over a medium heat for 3–4 minutes until just softened, stirring occasionally.

2

Add the tomatoes, garlic and herbs. Simmer, covered, for 30 minutes, then sieve the soup into a clean pan. Stir in the soured cream or yogurt and season. Reheat gently and serve garnished with cream or yogurt and marjoram.

Pumpkin Soup

When the first frosts of autumn chill the air, bright orange pumpkins are a vivid sight in gardens and at country markets. Pumpkin soup is delicious.

INGREDIENTS

25 g / 1 oz / 2 tbsp butter
1 large onion, chopped
2 shallots, chopped
2 potatoes, peeled and cubed
900 g / 2 lb / 6 cups cubed pumpkin flesh
2 litres / 3½ pints / 8 cups chicken or vegetable stock
½ tsp ground cumin
pinch of freshly grated nutmeg
salt and freshly ground black pepper
fresh parsley or chives, to garnish

Serves 6–8

1

Melt the butter in a large saucepan and cook the onion and shallots for 4–5 minutes until just softened. Add the potatoes, pumpkin, stock and spices, with a little salt and black pepper. Simmer, covered, for about 1 hour, stirring occasionally.

2

With a slotted spoon, transfer the cooked vegetables to a food processor. Process until smooth, adding a little of the cooking liquid if needed. Stir the purée into the cooking liquid remaining in the pan. Adjust the seasoning and reheat gently. Serve garnished with the fresh herbs.

Barley Soup

A feature of the farmhouse kitchen is the stockpot simmering on the stove. With a good home-made stock on hand, it only takes a few simple ingredients to make an excellent soup.

INGREDIENTS

900 g / 2 lb meaty bones (lamb, beef
or veal)
900 ml / 1½ pints / 3¾ cups water
30 ml / 2 tbsp oil
3 carrots, finely chopped
4 celery sticks, finely sliced
1 onion, finely chopped
30 ml / 2 tbsp pearl barley
salt and freshly ground black pepper

Serves 4

1

2

NOTE

All soups taste better with home-made stock. The long slow simmering can be done well in advance and stocks freeze well. A quick version of this soup can be made using water and a stock cube, but it won't have the same flavour.

Preheat the oven to 200°C / 400°F / Gas Mark 6. To prepare the meat stock, brown the lamb, beef or veal bones in a roasting tin in the oven for about 30 minutes. Put the bones in a large saucepan, cover with the water and bring to the boil.

Use a metal spoon to skim off the surface froth, then cover the pan and simmer the stock for at least 2 hours. Heat the oil in a saucepan and sauté the carrots, celery and onion for about 1 minute. Strain the stock into the pan.

3

Add the barley to the pan of vegetables and continue cooking for about 1 hour, until the barley is soft. Season the soup with plenty of salt and pepper, transfer to serving bowls and serve hot.

Bacon and Lentil Soup

Serve this hearty soup with chunks of warm, crusty bread.

INGREDIENTS

*450 g / 1 lb thick-sliced
bacon, cubed
1 onion, roughly chopped
1 small turnip, roughly chopped
1 celery stick, chopped
1 carrot, sliced
1 potato, peeled and
roughly chopped
75 g / 3 oz / ½ cup lentils
1 bouquet garni
freshly ground black pepper*

Serves 4

1

Heat a large pan and add the bacon. Cook for
a few minutes, allowing the fat to run out.

2

Add all the vegetables and cook for
4 minutes.

3

Add the lentils, bouquet garni, seasoning
and enough water to cover. Bring to the boil
and simmer for 1 hour, or until the lentils
are tender.

Stuffed Vine Leaves with Garlic Yogurt

This is the perfect starter to set the scene for one of those long summer lunches in the garden.

INGREDIENTS

225 g / 8 oz packet preserved vine leaves
1 onion, finely chopped
½ bunch spring onions, finely chopped
60 ml / 4 tbsp chopped fresh parsley
10 large fresh mint sprigs, chopped
finely grated rind of 1 lemon
½ tsp crushed dried chillies
7.5 ml / 1½ tsp fennel seeds, crushed
175 g / 6 oz / scant 1 cup long grain rice
120 ml / 4 fl oz / ½ cup olive oil
300 ml / ½ pint / 1¼ cups boiling water
150 ml / ¼ pint / ⅔ cup thick natural yogurt
2 garlic cloves, crushed
salt
lemon wedges and mint leaves, to garnish (optional)

Serves 6

1

Rinse the vine leaves well, then soak them in boiling water for 10 minutes. Meanwhile, mix the onion, spring onions, herbs, lemon rind, chillies, fennel seeds and rice with 25 ml / 1½ tbsp of the olive oil. Season with salt.

2

Drain the vine leaves. Place a vine leaf, veins uppermost, on a work surface and cut off any stalk. Place a heaped teaspoonful of the rice mixture near the stalk end. Fold the stalk end over the filling, then fold over the sides. Roll into a cigar shape. Repeat with the remaining leaves and filling.

3

Place any remaining leaves in the base of a heavy-based saucepan. Pack the stuffed leaves in a single layer in the pan. Spoon over the remaining oil, then add the measured boiling water.

4

Place a small plate over the leaves to keep them submerged. Cover and cook over a very low heat for 45 minutes. Meanwhile, mix the yogurt and garlic in a small serving dish. Transfer the stuffed leaves to a serving plate and garnish with lemon wedges and mint, if you like. Serve with the garlic yogurt.

Stuffed Garlic Mushrooms

Flavoursome field mushrooms make a simply delicious starter when stuffed and baked.

INGREDIENTS

1 onion, chopped
75 g / 3 oz / 6 tbsp butter
8 field mushrooms of similar size
15 g / ½ oz / ¼ cup dried mushrooms,
soaked in warm water for 20 minutes
1 garlic clove, crushed
75 g / 3 oz / 1½ cups fresh
breadcrumbs
1 egg
75 ml / 5 tbsp chopped fresh parsley
15 ml / 1 tbsp chopped fresh thyme
115 g / 4 oz prosciutto, thinly sliced
salt and freshly ground black pepper
fresh parsley, to garnish

Serves 4

1

Preheat the oven to 190°C / 375°F / Gas
Mark 5. Fry the onion gently in half the
butter until soft. Break off the stems of the
field mushrooms, setting the caps aside.
Drain the dried mushrooms and chop these
and the mushroom stems finely. Add to the
onion, with the garlic, and cook for
2–3 minutes more.

2

Tip the mixture into a bowl and add the
breadcrumbs, egg, herbs and seasoning.
Melt the remaining butter and brush it over
the mushroom caps. Arrange them on a
baking sheet and spoon in the filling. Bake
for 20–30 minutes until well browned. Top
each mushroom with a strip of prosciutto,
garnish with parsley and serve.

Mushroom Salad with Parma Ham

Ribbons of ham and pancake, tossed with wild mushrooms and salad leaves,
provide a feast for the eyes and the palate.

INGREDIENTS

40 g /1½ oz / 3 tbsp butter, plus extra
for greasing
450 g / 1 lb assorted wild and
cultivated mushrooms, sliced
60 ml / 4 tbsp sherry
juice of ½ lemon
mixed lettuce leaves
30 ml / 2 tbsp walnut oil
175 g / 6 oz Parma ham, cut into ribbons

For the pancake ribbons
25 g / 1 oz / ¼ cup plain flour
75 ml / 5 tbsp milk
1 egg
60 ml / 4 tbsp grated Parmesan cheese
60 ml / 4 tbsp chopped fresh herbs
salt and freshly ground black pepper

Serves 4

1

To make the pancake, mix the flour and
milk in a bowl. Beat in the egg, cheese,
herbs and seasoning. Pour enough of the
mixture into a hot, greased frying pan to
coat the bottom of it. When set, turn the
pancake over and cook briefly on the other
side. Cool, then roll up and slice into
ribbons. Repeat with the remaining batter.

2

Cook the mushrooms in the butter for
6–8 minutes. Add the sherry and lemon
juice, and season to taste.

3

Toss the lettuce in the oil and arrange on four
plates. Place the ham and pancake ribbons in the
centre and spoon on the mushrooms.

Mushroom Picker's Pâté

One of the delights of country living is to rise early and go on a mushrooming expedition with an expert who knows precisely what to pick. The pâté is the perfect reward.

INGREDIENTS

45 ml / 3 tbsp vegetable oil
1 onion, chopped
½ celery stick, chopped
350 g / 12 oz mushrooms, sliced
150 g / 5 oz / ⅔ cup red lentils
475 ml / 16 fl oz / 2 cups water or
vegetable stock
1 fresh thyme sprig

50 g / 2 oz / 4 tbsp almond nut butter
1 garlic clove, crushed
1 thick slice white bread, crusts removed
75 ml / 5 tbsp milk
15 ml / 1 tbsp lemon juice
4 egg yolks
celery salt and ground black pepper
Serves 6

1

Preheat the oven to 180°C / 350°F / Gas Mark 4. Brown the onion and celery in the oil. Add the mushrooms and soften for 3–4 minutes. Remove a spoonful of the mushroom pieces and set it aside.

2

Add the lentils, water or stock and thyme to the mushroom mixture. Bring to the boil, then lower the heat and simmer for 20 minutes or until the lentils are very soft.

3

Place the nut butter, garlic, bread and milk in a food processor and process until smooth.

4

Add the lemon juice and egg yolks and process briefly. Tip in the lentil mixture, process until smooth, then season with the celery salt and pepper. Lastly, stir the reserved mushrooms into the mixture.

5

Spoon the mixture into a 1.2 litre / 2 pint / 5 cup pâté dish and cover with foil. Stand the dish in a roasting tin and pour in boiling water to come halfway up the sides of the dish. Cook the pâté for 50 minutes. Allow to cool before serving.

NOTE
If you are using only cultivated mushrooms, an addition of 10 g / ⅓ oz / 3 tbsp of dried porcini will boost the flavour. Soak the dried mushrooms in warm water for 20 minutes before draining and adding to the pan with the fresh mushrooms.

Country-style Pâté with Leeks

A rough pâté is very much a feature of the farmhouse kitchen. Cooked slowly so that all the flavours combine, then pressed, it makes a perfect starter or light lunch.

INGREDIENTS

15 g / ½ oz / 1 tbsp butter
450 g / 1 lb leeks (white and pale green parts), sliced
2 or 3 large garlic cloves, finely chopped
1 kg / 2¼ lb lean pork leg or shoulder, trimmed and cubed
150 g / 5 oz rindless smoked streaky bacon rashers
7.5 ml / 1½ tsp chopped fresh thyme
3 fresh sage leaves, finely chopped
¼ tsp quatre épices (mixed ground cloves, cinnamon, nutmeg and black pepper)
¼ tsp ground cumin
pinch of freshly grated nutmeg
½ tsp salt
5 ml / 1 tsp freshly ground black pepper
1 bay leaf

Serves 8–10

1

Melt the butter in a large, heavy-based frying pan, add the leeks, then cover and sweat over a low heat for 10 minutes, stirring occasionally. Add the garlic and continue cooking for about 10 minutes until the leeks are very soft, then set aside to cool.

2

Pulse the meat cubes in batches in a food processor to chop it coarsely. Alternatively, pass the meat through the coarse blade of a mincer. Transfer the meat to a large mixing bowl and remove any white stringy bits. Reserve two of the bacon rashers for garnishing, then chop or grind the remainder, and mix with the pork in the mixing bowl.

3

Preheat the oven to 180°C / 350°F / Gas Mark 4. Line the base and sides of a 1.5 litre / 2½ pint / 6 cup terrine with greaseproof paper or baking parchment. Add the leek mixture, herbs and spices to the pork mixture, with the salt and pepper.

4

Spoon the mixture into the terrine, pressing it into the corners and compacting it. Tap firmly to settle the mixture and smooth the top. Arrange the bay leaf and bacon rashers on top, then cover tightly with foil.

5

Place the terrine in a roasting tin and pour in boiling water to come halfway up the side. Bake for 1¼ hours. Drain off the water, then return the terrine to the roasting tin and place a baking sheet on top. Weight with two or three large cans or a foil-wrapped clean house brick while the pâté cools. Chill overnight, before slicing.

Roasted Pepper Medley

When roasted, red peppers acquire a marvellous smoky flavour that is wonderful with sun-dried tomatoes and artichoke hearts.

INGREDIENTS

50 g / 2 oz / ½ cup drained sun-dried
tomatoes in oil
3 red peppers
2 yellow or orange peppers
2 green peppers
30 ml / 2 tbsp balsamic vinegar
a few drops of chilli sauce

75 ml / 5 tbsp olive oil
4 drained, canned artichoke hearts,
sliced
1 garlic clove, thinly sliced
salt and freshly ground black pepper
fresh basil leaves, to garnish

Serves 6

1

Preheat the oven to 200°C / 400°F / Gas
Mark 6. Slice the sun-dried tomatoes into
thin strips. Set aside. Put the whole
peppers on an oiled baking sheet and bake
for about 45 minutes until beginning to
char. Cover with a dish towel and leave to
cool for 5 minutes.

2

Mix the vinegar and chilli sauce in a bowl.
Whisk in the oil, then season with a little
salt and pepper.

3

Peel and slice the peppers. Mix with the
artichokes, tomatoes and garlic in a bowl.
Toss with the dressing and scatter with the
basil leaves.

Baby Aubergines with Raisins and Pine Nuts

Make this simple starter a day in advance, to allow the sour and sweet flavours to develop.

INGREDIENTS

*250 ml / 8 fl oz / 1 cup extra virgin
olive oil
juice of 1 lemon
30 ml / 2 tbsp balsamic vinegar
3 cloves
25 g / 1 oz / 1/3 cup pine nuts
25 g / 1 oz / 3 tbsp raisins
15 ml / 1 tbsp granulated sugar
1 bay leaf
large pinch of dried chilli flakes
12 baby aubergines, halved lengthways
salt and freshly ground black pepper*

Serves 4

TIP

Use sliced aubergines if baby ones are not
obtainable, or try this with grilled peppers.

1

Put 175 ml / 6 fl oz / ¾ cup of the olive oil
in a jug. Add the lemon juice, vinegar,
cloves, pine nuts, raisins, sugar and bay
leaf. Stir in the chilli flakes and salt and
pepper. Mix well. Preheat the grill.

2

Brush the aubergines with the remaining oil.
Grill for 10 minutes, until slightly blackened,
turning them over halfway through. Place the
hot aubergines in a bowl, and pour over the
marinade. Leave to cool, turning the
aubergines once or twice. Serve cold.

Cheese and Potato Patties

Serve these delicious little potato cakes with a simple tomato salad for an inexpensive but imaginative starter.

INGREDIENTS

500 g / 1¼ lb potatoes
115 g / 4 oz feta or Roquefort cheese
4 spring onions, finely chopped
45 ml / 3 tbsp chopped fresh dill
1 egg, beaten
15 ml / 1 tbsp lemon juice
plain flour, for dredging
45 ml / 3 tbsp olive oil
salt and freshly ground black pepper

Serves 4

TIP
Add salt sparingly when making the potato cakes, as the cheese will be salty.

1

Boil the potatoes in their skins in a saucepan of lightly salted water until soft. Drain, peel and mash while still warm. Crumble the feta cheese or Roquefort into the potatoes and add the spring onions, dill, egg and lemon juice. Season with salt and pepper. Stir well.

2

Cover the mixture and chill until firm. Divide the mixture into walnut-sized balls, then flatten them slightly. Dredge with flour. Heat the oil in a frying pan and fry the potato patties until golden brown on each side. Drain on kitchen paper and serve at once.

Fonduta

Fontina is an Italian medium-fat cheese with a rich salty flavour, a little like Gruyère, which makes a good substitute. This delicious hot dip makes a good starter before a fairly light main course. Serve it with warm crusty bread.

INGREDIENTS

250 g / 9 oz fontina or Gruyère
cheese, diced
250 ml / 8 fl oz / 1 cup milk
15 g / ½ oz / 1 tbsp butter
2 eggs, lightly beaten
freshly ground black pepper

Serves 4

NOTE
Do not overheat the sauce, or the eggs may curdle. A very gentle heat will produce a lovely smooth sauce.

1

Put the cheese in a bowl with the milk and leave to soak for 2–3 hours. Transfer to a double boiler or a heatproof bowl set over a pan of simmering water.

2

Add the butter and eggs and stir gently until the cheese has melted to a smooth sauce. Remove from the heat, season with pepper and serve in a warmed serving dish.

Vegetables

Farmhouse cooks really know their vegetables. They tend to cook by the season, picking or pulling up the first young vegetables as soon as they are ready, and turning them into superb side dishes, salads and vegetarian meals. The following section is a selection of delicious recipes inspired by the rural tradition. Some of the recipes are for hearty main dishes, while others are designed as flavoursome side dishes. All rely on the use of the freshest possible vegetables, so to help guarantee the best results avoid using limp specimens.

Stuffed Parsleyed Onions

*Although devised as a vegetarian dish, these stuffed onions make a wonderful
accompaniment to meat dishes, or an appetizing supper dish with crusty bread and a salad.*

INGREDIENTS

4 large onions
4 tbsp cooked rice
4 tsp finely chopped fresh parsley,
plus extra to garnish
4 tbsp strong Cheddar cheese, finely
grated
salt and pepper
2 tbsp olive oil
1 tbsp white wine, to moisten

Serves 4

1

Cut a slice from the top of each onion and
scoop out the centre to leave a thick shell.

2

Combine all the remaining ingredients,
moistening with enough wine to mix well.
Preheat the oven to 180°C/350°F/
Gas Mark 4.

3

Fill the onions and bake in the oven for
45 minutes. Serve garnished with parsley.

Stuffed Tomatoes, with Wild Rice, Corn and Coriander

These tomatoes could be served as a light meal or as an accompaniment for meat or fish.

INGREDIENTS

8 medium tomatoes
50g / 2oz sweetcorn kernels
2 tbsp white wine
50g / 2oz cooked wild rice
1 clove garlic
50g / 2oz grated Cheddar cheese
1 tbsp chopped fresh coriander
salt and pepper
1 tbsp olive oil

Serves 4

1

Cut the tops off the tomatoes and remove the seeds with a small teaspoon. Scoop out all the flesh and chop finely – remember to chop the tops as well.

2

Preheat the oven to 180°C/350°F/Gas Mark 4. Put the chopped tomato in a pan. Add the sweetcorn and the white wine. Cover with a close-fitting lid and simmer until tender. Drain the excess liquid.

3

Mix together all the remaining ingredients except the olive oil, adding salt and pepper to taste. Carefully spoon the mixture into the tomatoes, piling it higher in the centre. Sprinkle the oil over the top, arrange the tomatoes in an ovenproof dish and bake at 180°C/350°F/Gas Mark 4 for 15–20 minutes until cooked through.

Garden Salad

You can use any fresh, edible flowers from your garden for this beautiful salad.

INGREDIENTS

1 cos lettuce
175 g / 6 oz rocket
1 small frisée lettuce
fresh chervil and tarragon sprigs
15 ml / 1 tbsp snipped fresh chives
handful of mixed edible flower
heads, such as nasturtiums
or marigolds

For the dressing
45 ml / 3 tbsp olive oil
15 ml / 1 tbsp white-wine vinegar
½ tsp French mustard
1 garlic clove, crushed
pinch of sugar

Serves 4

___1___

Mix the cos, rocket and frisée leaves
and herbs together.

___2___

Make the dressing by whisking all the
ingredients together in a large bowl. Toss the
salad leaves in the bowl with the dressing,
add the flower heads and serve at once.

Creamy Layered Potatoes

Cook the potatoes on the hob first to help the dish to bake more quickly.

INGREDIENTS

1.5 kg / 3–3½ lb large potatoes,
peeled and sliced
2 large onions, sliced
75 g / 3 oz / 6 tbsp unsalted butter
300 ml / ½ pint / 1¼ cups double
cream
salt and freshly ground
black pepper

Serves 6

___2___

Transfer to an ovenproof dish, season and bake for 1 hour, until the potatoes are tender.

___1___

Preheat the oven to 200°C / 400°F / Gas Mark 6. Blanch the sliced potatoes for 2 minutes, and drain well. Place the potatoes, onions, butter and cream in a large pan, stir well and cook for about 15 minutes.

New Potato Salad

Potatoes freshly dug up from the garden are the best. Always leave the skins on: just wash the dirt away thoroughly. If you add the mayonnaise and other ingredients when the potatoes are hot, the flavours will develop as the potatoes cool.

INGREDIENTS

900 g / 2 lb baby new potatoes
2 green apples, cored and chopped
4 spring onions, chopped
3 celery sticks, finely chopped
150 ml / ¼ pint / ⅔ cup
mayonnaise
salt and freshly ground
black pepper

Serves 6

1

Cook the potatoes in salted, boiling water for about 20 minutes, or until they are very tender.

2

Drain the potatoes well and immediately add the remaining ingredients and stir until well mixed. Leave to cool and serve cold.

French Bean Salad

The secret of this recipe is to dress the beans while still hot.

INGREDIENTS

175 g / 6 oz cherry tomatoes,
halved
5 ml / 1 tsp sugar
450 g / 1 lb French beans,
topped and tailed
175 g / 6 oz feta cheese, cubed
salt and freshly ground
black pepper

For the dressing
90 ml / 6 tbsp olive oil
45 ml / 3 tbsp white-wine vinegar
¼ tsp Dijon mustard
2 garlic cloves, crushed
salt and freshly ground
black pepper

Serves 6

1

Preheat the oven to 230°C / 450°F / Gas Mark 8. Put the cherry tomatoes on a baking sheet and sprinkle over the sugar, salt and pepper. Roast for 10 minutes, then leave to cool. Meanwhile, cook the beans in boiling, salted water for 10 minutes.

2

Make the dressing by whisking together the oil, vinegar, mustard, garlic and seasoning. Drain the beans and immediately pour over the vinaigrette and mix well. When cool, stir in the roasted tomatoes and the feta cheese. Serve chilled.

Rosemary Roasties

These unusual roast potatoes use far less fat than conventional roast potatoes, and because they still have their skins they have more flavour too.

INGREDIENTS

1 kg / 2¼ lb small red potatoes
10 ml / 2 tsp walnut or sunflower oil
30 ml / 2 tbsp fresh rosemary leaves
salt and paprika

Serves 4

NOTE
This is also delicious with tiny salad potatoes, especially if you roast them with chunks of red onion.

1

Preheat the oven to 240°C / 475°F / Gas Mark 9. Scrub the potatoes. If they are large, cut them in half. Place in a pan of cold water and bring to the boil. Drain.

2

Drizzle the oil over the potatoes and shake the pan to coat them evenly.

3

Tip the potatoes into a shallow roasting tin. Sprinkle with the rosemary, salt and paprika. Roast for 30–45 minutes. Serve hot.

Baked Courgettes in Tomato Sauce

Courgettes and tomatoes have a natural affinity. Use fresh tomatoes, cooked and puréed, instead of passata if possible.

INGREDIENTS

5 ml / 1 tsp olive oil
3 large courgettes, thinly sliced
½ small red onion, finely chopped
300 ml / ½ pint / 1¼ cups passata
(puréed tomatoes)
30 ml / 2 tbsp chopped fresh thyme
garlic salt and freshly ground black
pepper
fresh thyme sprigs, to garnish

Serves 4

1

Preheat the oven to 190°C / 375°F / Gas Mark 5. Brush a baking dish with olive oil. Arrange half the courgettes and onion in the dish.

2

Spoon half the passata over the vegetables. Sprinkle with some of the fresh thyme, then season to taste with garlic salt and pepper. Repeat with the remaining ingredients. Cover the dish and bake for 40–45 minutes. Garnish with thyme sprigs and serve hot.

Spicy Fried Potatoes

Give fried potatoes a hint of heat by tossing them with spiced vinegar.
Sliced peppers add a splash of colour.

INGREDIENTS

2 garlic cloves, sliced
½ tsp crushed chillies
½ tsp ground cumin
10 ml / 2 tsp paprika
30 ml / 2 tbsp red or white wine
vinegar
675 g / 1½ lb small new potatoes
75 ml / 5 tbsp olive oil
1 red or green pepper, seeded and sliced
coarse sea salt, to serve (optional)

Serves 4

1

Mix the garlic, chillies and cumin in a mortar. Crush with a pestle, then stir in the paprika and wine vinegar.

2

Bring a saucepan of lightly salted water to the boil and cook the potatoes, in their skins, for about 15 minutes until almost tender. Drain, peel, if preferred, and cut into chunks. Heat the oil in a large frying pan; sauté the potatoes until golden.

3

Add the spiced garlic mixture to the potatoes with the sliced pepper and continue to cook, stirring, for 2 minutes. Serve warm, or leave until cold. Scatter with coarse sea salt, if you like, to serve.

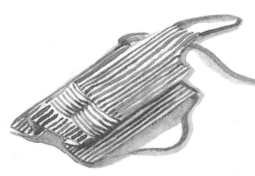

Turnip Tops with Parmesan and Garlic

Farmhouse cooks know how to turn everyday ingredients into treats. Here, turnip tops are flavoured with onions, garlic and Parmesan cheese. They do not need long cooking as the leaves are quite tender.

INGREDIENTS

45 ml / 3 tbsp olive oil
2 garlic cloves, crushed
4 spring onions, sliced
350 g / 12 oz turnip tops, thinly sliced, tough stalks removed
60 ml / 4 tbsp water
50 g / 2 oz / ⅔ cup grated Parmesan cheese
salt and freshly ground black pepper
shavings of Parmesan cheese, to garnish

Serves 4

1

Heat the olive oil in a large saucepan and stir-fry the garlic and spring onions for 2 minutes. Add the turnip tops and stir-fry for 2–3 minutes so that the greens are coated in oil. Add the water.

2

Bring to the boil, lower the heat, cover and simmer, stirring frequently, until the greens are tender. Bring the liquid to the boil again, allow the excess to evaporate, then stir in the Parmesan and seasoning. Serve at once with extra shavings of cheese.

Spiced Turnips with Spinach and Tomatoes

Sweet baby turnips, tender spinach and ripe tomatoes make tempting partners in this simple vegetable stew.

INGREDIENTS

450 g / 1 lb well-flavoured tomatoes
60 ml / 4 tbsp olive oil
2 onions, chopped or sliced
450 g / 1 lb baby turnips, peeled
5 ml / 1 tsp paprika
60 ml / 4 tbsp water
2.5 ml / ½ tsp caster sugar
60 ml / 4 tbsp chopped fresh coriander
450 g / 1 lb fresh young spinach, stalks removed
salt and freshly ground black pepper

Serves 6

1

Plunge the tomatoes into a bowl of boiling water for 30 seconds, then refresh in a bowl of cold water. Peel away the tomato skins and chop roughly.

2

Heat the olive oil in a large frying pan and fry the onion for about 5 minutes until golden. Add the baby turnips, tomatoes, paprika and water to the pan and cook until the tomatoes are pulpy. Cover and continue cooking until the baby turnips are soft.

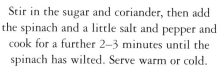

3

Stir in the sugar and coriander, then add the spinach and a little salt and pepper and cook for a further 2–3 minutes until the spinach has wilted. Serve warm or cold.

Salsify and Spinach Bake

The spinach in this recipe adds colour and makes it go further. However, if you have plenty of salsify, plus the patience to peel it, increase the quantity and leave out the spinach.

INGREDIENTS

juice of 2 lemons
450 g / 1 lb salsify
450 g / 1 lb fresh spinach leaves
150 ml / ¼ pint / ⅔ cup chicken or vegetable stock
300 ml / ½ pint / 1¼ cups single cream
salt and freshly ground black pepper

Serves 4

2

Meanwhile, cook the spinach in a large saucepan over a medium heat for 2–3 minutes until the leaves have wilted, shaking the pan occasionally. Place the stock, cream and seasoning in a small saucepan and heat through very gently, stirring.

3

Grease a baking dish generously with butter. Drain the salsify and spinach and arrange in layers in the prepared dish. Pour over the stock and cream mixture and bake for about 1 hour until the top is golden brown and bubbling.

1

Preheat the oven to 160°C / 325°F / Gas Mark 3. Add a quarter of the lemon juice to a large bowl of water. Top, tail and peel the salsify. Place each peeled root immediately in the acidulated water, to prevent discoloration. Bring a saucepan of water to the boil. Add the remaining lemon juice. Cut the salsify into 5 cm / 2 in lengths, add it to the pan and simmer for about 10 minutes, until just tender.

Glazed Carrots with Cider

Cooking young carrots with the minimum of liquid brings out the best of their flavour, and the cider adds a pleasant sharpness.

INGREDIENTS

450 g / 1 lb young carrots
25 g / 1 oz / 2 tbsp butter
15 ml / 1 tbsp soft brown sugar
120 ml / 4 fl oz / ½ cup cider
60 ml / 4 tbsp vegetable stock
5 ml / 1 tsp Dijon mustard
15 ml / 1 tbsp finely chopped fresh parsley

Serves 4

NOTE
If the carrots are cooked before the liquid in the frying pan has reduced, transfer the carrots to a serving dish and rapidly boil the liquid until thick. Pour the liquid over the carrots and sprinkle with parsley.

1

Trim the tops and bottoms of the carrots. Peel or scrape them. Using a sharp knife, cut them into matchstick strips. Melt the butter in a frying pan and sauté the carrots for 4–5 minutes.

2

Sprinkle over the sugar and cook, stirring, for 1 minute. Add the cider and stock, bring to the boil and stir in the mustard. Partially cover the pan and simmer for 10–12 minutes until the carrots are just tender. Remove the lid and continue cooking until the liquid has reduced to a thick sauce. Toss the carrots with the parsley and spoon into a warmed serving dish.

Carrot, Apple and Orange Coleslaw

This dish is as delicious as it is easy to make. The garlic and herb dressing adds the necessary contrast to the sweetness of the salad.

INGREDIENTS

350 g / 12 oz young carrots, finely grated
2 eating apples
15 ml / 1 tbsp lemon juice
1 large orange, peeled and segmented

For the dressing
45 ml / 3 tbsp olive oil
60 ml / 4 tbsp sunflower oil
45 ml / 3 tbsp lemon juice
1 garlic clove, crushed
60 ml / 4 tbsp natural yogurt
15 ml / 1 tbsp chopped mixed fresh herbs
salt and freshly ground black pepper

Serves 4

1

Place the carrots in a large serving bowl. Quarter the apples, remove the core from each wedge and then slice thinly. Sprinkle the apples with lemon juice to prevent discoloration, then add to the carrots, with the orange segments.

2

To make the dressing, place the oils, lemon juice and garlic in a jar with a tight-fitting lid and shake vigorously. Add the remaining ingredients and shake again. Just before serving, pour the dressing over the salad and toss well.

Brussels Sprouts with Chestnuts

A traditional Christmas speciality, this combination of crisp, tender Brussels sprouts and chestnuts is perennially popular.

INGREDIENTS

225 g / 8 oz chestnuts
120 ml / 4 fl oz / ½ cup milk
500 g / 1¼ lb / 4 cups small tender Brussels sprouts
25 g / 1 oz / 2 tbsp butter
1 shallot, finely chopped
30–45 ml / 2–3 tbsp dry white wine or water

Serves 4–6

1

Cut a cross in the base of each chestnut. Bring a saucepan of water to the boil, drop in the chestnuts and boil for 6–8 minutes. Peel while still warm, then return to the clean pan. Add the milk and enough water to cover the chestnuts. Simmer for 12–15 minutes. Drain and set aside.

2

Remove any wilted or yellow leaves from the Brussels sprouts. Trim the root end but leave intact or the leaves will separate. Using a small knife, cut a cross in the base of each sprout.

3

Melt the butter in a large, heavy-based frying pan, and cook the shallot for 1–2 minutes until just softened. Add the Brussels sprouts and wine or water. Cover and cook over a medium heat for 6–8 minutes, shaking the pan occasionally and adding a little more water if necessary.

4

Add the poached chestnuts and toss gently, then cover and cook for 3–5 minutes more. Serve at once.

Leeks in Egg and Lemon Sauce

*Tender young leeks, picked fresh from the vegetable plot, cooked and cooled
in a tart creamy sauce, taste absolutely superb.*

*675 g / 1½ lb baby leeks, trimmed,
slit and washed
15 ml / 1 tbsp cornflour
10 ml / 2 tsp sugar
2 egg yolks
juice of 1½ lemons
salt*

Serves 4

3

Whisk the egg yolks with the lemon juice
and stir gradually into the cooled sauce.
Cook over a very low heat, stirring all the
time, until the sauce is fairly thick.
Immediately remove from the heat and
continue stirring for 1 minute. Taste and
add salt or sugar as necessary. Cool slightly.

4

Pour the sauce over the leeks. Cover and
chill for at least 2 hours before serving.

NOTE
Do not let the sauce overheat after adding
the egg yolks or it may curdle.

1

Lay the leeks flat in a large saucepan, cover
with water and add a little salt. Bring to
the boil, lower the heat, cover and simmer
for 4–5 minutes until just tender.

2

Lift out the leeks, drain well and arrange in
a shallow serving dish. Mix 200 ml / 7 fl
oz / scant 1 cup of the cooking liquid with
the cornflour in a saucepan. Bring to the
boil, stirring all the time, then cook until
the sauce thickens slightly. Stir in the
sugar. Cool slightly.

Peas with Lettuce and Onion

Podding peas is a traditional pastime in the farmhouse kitchen. Sweet young peas taste delicious when cooked with strips of lettuce.

INGREDIENTS

15 g / ½ oz / 1 tbsp butter
1 small onion, finely chopped
1 small round lettuce, halved and
sliced into thin strips
450 g / 1 lb / 3½ cups shelled fresh
peas (from about 1.5 kg / 3½ lb pods),
or thawed frozen peas
45 ml / 3 tbsp water
salt and freshly ground black pepper

Serves 4–6

1

Melt the butter in a heavy-based saucepan.
Add the onion and cook over a medium-
low heat for about 3 minutes until just
softened. Place the lettuce strips on top of
the onion and add the peas and water.
Season lightly with salt and pepper.

2

Cover the pan tightly and cook the lettuce
and peas over a low heat until the peas are
tender – fresh peas will take 10–20
minutes, frozen peas about 10 minutes.
Toss lightly and serve at once.

Broad Beans with Cream

Skinned broad beans are a beautiful bright green. Try this simple way of serving them.

INGREDIENTS

450 g/1 lb shelled broad beans (from
about 2 kg / 4½ lb pods)
90 ml / 6 tbsp crème fraîche or
whipping cream
salt and freshly ground black pepper
finely snipped chives, to garnish

Serves 4–6

1

Bring a large pan of lightly salted water to
the boil and add the beans. Reduce the heat
slightly and cook the beans for about
8 minutes until just tender. Drain, refresh
under cold running water, then drain again.

2

Remove the skins by slitting each bean and
gently squeezing out the kernel.

NOTE

If you can find them, fresh flageolet or lima
beans can be served in the same way.

3

Put the skinned beans in a saucepan with
the cream and seasoning, cover and heat
through gently. Sprinkle with the snipped
chives and serve at once.

Baked Beans with Sage

Sage is a somewhat neglected herb, used for stuffings and liver dishes, but little else. It gives baked beans an incomparable flavour.

INGREDIENTS

600 g / 1 lb 6 oz / 3¼ cups dried
beans, such as cannellini
60 ml / 4 tbsp olive oil
2 garlic cloves, crushed
3 fresh sage leaves
1 leek, finely sliced
400 g / 14 oz can chopped tomatoes
salt and freshly ground black pepper

Serves 6–8

1

Carefully pick over the beans, discarding any stones or other particles. Place the beans in a bowl and cover with water. Soak for at least 6 hours, or overnight. Drain.

2

Preheat the oven to 180°C / 350°F / Gas Mark 4. Heat the oil in a small saucepan and sauté the garlic cloves and sage leaves for 3–4 minutes. Remove from the heat.

3

Put the beans in a large, deep baking dish and add the leek and tomatoes. Stir in the oil with the garlic and sage. Add enough fresh water to cover the beans by 2.5 cm / 1 in. Mix well. Cover the dish and bake for 1¾ hours.

4

Remove the dish from the oven, stir the beans, and season with salt and pepper. Return the dish to the oven, uncovered, and cook the beans for 15 minutes more, or until tender. Remove from the oven and allow to stand for 7–8 minutes before serving.

Squash à la Greque

A traditional French-style dish that is usually made with mushrooms. Make sure that you cook the baby squash until they are quite tender, so they can fully absorb the delicious flavours of the marinade.

INGREDIENTS

175 g / 6 oz patty-pan squash
250 ml / 8 fl oz / 1 cup white wine
juice of 2 lemons
fresh thyme sprig
bay leaf
small bunch of fresh chervil,
roughly chopped
¼ tsp coriander seeds, crushed
¼ tsp black peppercorns, crushed
75 ml / 5 tbsp olive oil

Serves 4

1

Blanch the patty-pan squash in boiling water for 3 minutes, and then refresh them in cold water.

2

Place all the remaining ingredients in a pan, add 150 ml / ½ pint / ⅔ cup of water and simmer for 10 minutes, covered. Add the patty-pans and cook for 10 minutes. Remove with a slotted spoon when they are cooked and tender to the bite.

3

Reduce the liquid by boiling hard for 10 minutes. Strain it and pour it over the squashes. Leave until cool for the flavours to be absorbed. Serve cold.

Aubergines with Garlic and Tomato Glaze

An unusual way of cooking aubergines, which tend to absorb large amounts of oil when fried. Roasting the slices in the oven makes them slightly crisp.

INGREDIENTS

2 aubergines, about 225 g / 8 oz each, sliced
2 garlic cloves, crushed
45 ml / 3 tbsp tomato purée
90–120 ml / 6–8 tbsp olive oil
½ tsp granulated sugar
salt and freshly ground black pepper
chopped flat leaf parsley, to garnish

Serves 2–4

1

Spread out the aubergines on kitchen paper. Sprinkle them with salt and leave for about 30 minutes. Meanwhile, preheat the oven to 190°C / 375°F / Gas Mark 5. Mix the garlic and tomato purée with 15 ml / 1 tbsp of the oil in a bowl. Add the sugar, salt and pepper.

2

Rinse, drain and dry the aubergine slices. Pour about 60 ml / 4 tbsp of the oil into a baking tin and arrange the aubergine slices in a single layer. Spoon a little of the garlic tomato mixture over each one. Drizzle over the remaining oil, then bake for about 30 minutes. Arrange on a flat dish, garnish with chopped parsley and serve.

Beetroot with Soured Cream

Freshly lifted from the farmhouse garden, small beetroot make a delicious snack or side dish when simply boiled and served with soured cream.

INGREDIENTS

450 g / 1 lb small uncooked beetroot
300 ml / ½ pint / 1¼ cups chilled soured cream
salt and freshly ground black pepper
fresh dill sprigs, to garnish

Serves 4

NOTE

To prepare the beetroot, cut off the leaves about 2.5 cm/1 in from the tops and remove the thin roots. Wash the beetroot very well, removing any dirt with a vegetable brush. Take care not to cut the beetroot or the colour will leach out.

1

Put the beetroot in a saucepan with water to cover generously. Season well, bring to the boil and simmer for 30–40 minutes. Drain the beetroot, and while they are still warm, use a knife to peel off the skin.

2

Spoon the chilled soured cream on to individual plates. Cut the beetroot into wedges and use one to make a pretty pink swirl. Arrange the wedges around the plates and garnish with dill sprigs.

Globe Artichokes with Green Beans and Aïoli

Gloriously garlicky aïoli is the perfect partner for freshly cooked vegetables.

INGREDIENTS

225 g / 8 oz green beans
3 small globe artichokes
15 ml / 1 tbsp olive oil
pared rind of 1 lemon
coarse salt for sprinkling
lemon wedges, to garnish

For the aïoli
6 large garlic cloves
10 ml / 2 tsp white wine vinegar
250 ml / 8 fl oz / 1 cup olive oil
salt and freshly ground black pepper

Serves 4–6

NOTE
If you prefer to make the aïoli by hand,
crush the garlic with the vinegar, then
gradually whisk in the oil.

1

Make the aïoli. Crush the garlic with the
flat blade of a cook's knife. Put it in a
blender and add the vinegar. Blend to a
paste. With the machine switched on,
gradually pour in the olive oil through the
feed-tube until the mixture is thick and
smooth. Season with salt and pepper
to taste.

2

Cook the beans in a large saucepan of
lightly salted boiling water for
1–2 minutes until they have softened
slightly. Remove from the water with a
slotted spoon and set aside. Trim the
artichoke stalks close to the base. Add the
artichokes to the pan of boiling water and
cook for about 30 minutes, or until you can
easily pull away a leaf from the base.
Drain well.

3

Using a sharp knife, cut the artichokes in
half lengthways and ease out the choke
using a teaspoon. Arrange the artichokes
and beans on serving plates and drizzle
with the oil. Scatter with the lemon rind
and season with coarse salt and a little
pepper. Spoon the aïoli into the artichoke
hearts and serve warm, garnished with the
lemon wedges.

Stewed Artichokes

*There are lots of wonderful ways to serve artichokes. Try them lightly
stewed with garlic, parsley and wine.*

INGREDIENTS

1 lemon
4 large or 6 small globe artichokes
25 g / 1 oz / 2 tbsp butter
60 ml / 4 tbsp olive oil
2 garlic cloves, finely chopped
60 ml / 4 tbsp chopped fresh parsley
45 ml / 3 tbsp water
90 ml / 6 tbsp milk
90 ml / 6 tbsp white wine
salt and freshly ground black pepper

Serves 6

1

Squeeze the lemon juice into a large bowl of
cold water. Put a large pan of water on the
stove and bring to the boil while you
prepare the artichokes one at a time.

2

Cut off the tip from the artichoke's stem.
Peel the stem, pulling off the small leaves
around it, and continue until you reach the
taller inner leaves. Slice off the topmost part
of the leaves. Cut the artichoke into
segments, then cut out the choke from each
segment. Place the artichokes in the
acidulated water, then blanch in the boiling
water for 4–5 minutes. Drain well.

3

Heat the butter and olive oil in a large
saucepan and fry the garlic and parsley for
2–3 minutes. Stir in the artichokes, water
and milk, season, then cook for 10 minutes,
or until the liquid has evaporated. Stir in
the wine, cover and cook until the
artichokes are tender. Serve hot or at
room temperature.

Green Beans with Tomatoes

Green beans in a rich tomato sauce make a dish that is as colourful as it is good to eat.

INGREDIENTS

45 ml / 3 tbsp olive oil
*1 onion, preferably red, very finely
sliced*
*350 g / 12 oz plum tomatoes, peeled
and finely chopped*
120 ml / 4 fl oz / ½ cup water
5–6 fresh basil leaves, torn into shreds
*450 g / 1 lb fresh green beans,
trimmed*
salt and freshly ground black pepper

Serves 4–6

1

Heat the oil in a large frying pan. Add the
onion slices and cook for 5–6 minutes,
until just soft. Add the tomatoes and cook
over a medium heat for 6–8 minutes, until
they soften. Stir in the water. Season with
salt and pepper, and add the basil.

2

Stir in the beans, turning them in the pan
to coat them with the sauce. Cover the pan,
and cook over a medium heat for 15–20
minutes, until tender. Stir occasionally, and
add a little more water if the sauce dries
out too much. Serve hot or cold.

Leek Tart

This unusual recipe isn't a normal tart with pastry, but an all-in-one savoury slice that is excellent served as an accompaniment to roast meat.

INGREDIENTS

50 g / 2 oz / 4 tbsp unsalted butter
350 g / 12 oz leeks, sliced thinly
225 g / 8 oz / 2 cups self-raising flour
115 g / 4 oz / ½ cup grated hard white fat
150 ml / ¼ pint / ⅔ cup water
salt and freshly ground black pepper

Serves 4

1

Preheat the oven to 200°C / 400°F / Gas Mark 6. Melt the butter in a pan and sauté the leeks until soft. Season well.

2

Mix the flour, fat and water together in a bowl to make a soft but sticky dough. Mix into the leek mixture in the pan. Place in a greased shallow ovenproof dish and bake for 30 minutes, or until brown and crispy. Serve sliced, as a vegetable accompaniment.

Braised Red Cabbage

The combination of red wine vinegar and sugar gives this dish a sweet, yet tart flavour. In France it is often served with game, but it is also delicious with pork, duck or cold meats.

INGREDIENTS

30 ml / 2 tbsp vegetable oil
2 onions, thinly sliced
2 eating apples, peeled, cored and thinly sliced
1 head red cabbage (about 900 g / 2 lb), trimmed, cored, halved and thinly sliced
60 ml / 4 tbsp red wine vinegar
15–30 ml / 1–2 tbsp granulated sugar
¼ tsp ground cloves
5–10 ml / 1–2 tsp mustard seeds
50 g / 2 oz / ⅓ cup raisins or currants
about 120 ml / 4 fl oz / ½ cup red wine or water
15–30 ml / 1–2 tbsp redcurrant jelly
salt and freshly ground black pepper

Serves 6–8

1

Heat the oil in a large, stainless steel saucepan over a medium heat. Fry the onions for 7–10 minutes until golden. Stir in the apples and cook, stirring, for 2–3 minutes until they are just softened.

2

Add the cabbage, red wine vinegar, sugar, cloves, mustard seeds, raisins or currants, red wine or water and salt and pepper, stirring until well mixed. Bring to the boil, stirring occasionally.

3

Cover and cook over a fairly low heat for 35–40 minutes until the cabbage is tender and the liquid is just absorbed, stirring occasionally. Add a little more red wine or water if the pan boils dry before the cabbage is tender. Just before serving, stir in the redcurrant jelly to sweeten and glaze the cabbage.

Eggs and Cheese

Baskets of eggs and truckles of cheese invite experimentation. These simple ingredients form the basis of a wide range of delicious dishes, most of which can be made in moments. Use free-range eggs and farmhouse cheeses, which are now readily available from supermarkets, for the best possible flavour. The following section shows just how versatile and appetizing eggs and cheese are. The recipes themselves are all fairly straightforward but the end results are all positively mouth-watering.

Carrot and Coriander Soufflés

Use tender young carrots for this light-as-air dish.

INGREDIENTS

450 g / 1 lb carrots
30 ml / 2 tbsp fresh chopped coriander
4 eggs, separated
salt and freshly ground black pepper

Serves 4

1

Peel the carrots.

2

Cook in boiling salted water for 20 minutes or until tender. Drain, and process until smooth in a food processor.

3

Preheat the oven to 200°C / 400°F / Gas Mark 6. Season the puréed carrots well, and stir in the chopped coriander.

4

Fold the egg yolks into the carrot mixture.

5

In a separate bowl, whisk the egg whites until stiff.

6

Fold the egg whites into the carrot mixture and pour into four greased ramekins. Bake for about 20 minutes or until risen and golden. Serve immediately.

Mediterranean Quiche

The strong Mediterranean flavours of tomatoes, peppers and anchovies
complement beautifully the cheesy pastry in this unusual quiche.

INGREDIENTS

For the pastry
225 g / 8 oz / 2 cups plain flour
pinch of salt
pinch of dry mustard
115 g / 4 oz / ½ cup butter,
chilled and cubed
50 g / 2 oz Gruyère cheese, grated

For the filling
50 g / 2 oz can of anchovies in oil,
drained
50 ml / 2 fl oz / ¼ cup milk
30 ml / 2 tbsp French mustard
45 ml / 3 tbsp olive oil
2 large Spanish onions, sliced
1 red pepper, seeded and
very finely sliced
3 egg yolks
350 ml / 12 fl oz / 1½ cups
double cream
1 garlic clove, crushed
175 g / 6 oz mature Cheddar
cheese, grated
2 large tomatoes, thickly sliced
salt and freshly ground
black pepper
30 ml / 2 tbsp chopped fresh basil,
to garnish

Serves 8

1

First make the pastry. Place the flour, salt
and mustard powder in a food processor,
add the butter and process the mixture
until it resembles breadcrumbs.

2

Add the cheese and process again briefly.
Add enough iced water to make a stiff dough:
it will be ready when the dough forms a ball.
Wrap with cling film and chill for 30 minutes.

3

Meanwhile, make the filling. Soak the
anchovies in the milk for 20 minutes.
Drain away the milk.

4

Roll out the chilled pastry and line a 23 cm /
9 in loose-based flan tin. Spread over the
mustard and chill for a further 15 minutes.

5

Preheat the oven to 200°C / 400°F /
Gas Mark 6. Heat the oil in a frying pan and
cook the onions and red pepper until soft.
In a separate bowl, beat the egg yolks,
cream, garlic and Cheddar cheese together;
season well. Arrange the tomatoes in a
single layer in the pastry case. Top with the
onion and pepper mixture and the anchovy
fillets. Pour over the egg mixture.
Bake for 30–35 minutes. Sprinkle over
the basil and serve.

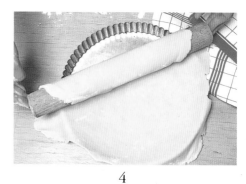

Cheese and Bacon Quiche

Quiches are great country fare, ideal for al fresco meals. To pack for a picnic, double wrap the tin in foil and support it in a stout box.

INGREDIENTS

350 g / 12 oz shortcrust pastry,
thawed if frozen
15 ml / 1 tbsp Dijon mustard
175 g / 6 oz / 6 rindless streaky
bacon rashers, chopped
3 eggs
350 ml / 12 fl oz / 1½ cups single cream
1 onion, chopped
150 g / 5 oz Gruyère cheese, diced
salt and freshly ground black pepper
fresh parsley, to garnish

Serves 6–8

1

Preheat the oven to 200°C / 400°F / Gas Mark 6. Roll out the pastry and line a 23 cm / 9 in flan tin. Prick the base of the pastry case and bake for 15 minutes. Brush the case with mustard and bake for 5 minutes more. Reduce the oven temperature to 180°C / 350°F / Gas Mark 4.

2

Fry the bacon until crisp and browned. Beat the eggs and cream, season with salt and pepper and set aside.

3

Drain the bacon. Pour off most of the fat from the pan, add the onion and cook gently for about 15 minutes.

4

Sprinkle half the cheese over the pastry, then the onion, followed by the bacon and remaining cheese. Pour on the egg mixture and bake for 35–45 minutes until set. Serve warm, garnished with parsley.

Chard Omelette

This traditional flat omelette can also be made with fresh spinach, but the large leaves of Swiss chard – a variety of white beet – are more authentic.

INGREDIENTS

675 g / 1½ lb Swiss chard leaves,
without stalks
60 ml / 4 tbsp olive oil
1 large onion, sliced
5 eggs
salt and freshly ground black pepper
fresh parsley sprig, to garnish

Serves 6

1

Wash the chard well in several changes of water and pat dry. Stack four or five leaves at a time and slice across into thin ribbons. Steam the chard until wilted, then drain in a sieve and press out any liquid with the back of a spoon.

2

Heat half the olive oil in a large frying pan. Add the onion and cook over a medium-low heat for about 10 minutes until soft, stirring occasionally. Add the chard and cook for a further 2–4 minutes until the leaves are tender.

3

Beat the eggs in a large bowl. Season with salt and pepper, then stir in the cooked vegetables. Heat the remaining oil in a large frying pan, pour in the egg mixture and reduce the heat to medium-low. Cook the omelette, covered, for 5–7 minutes until the egg mixture is set around the edges and almost set on top.

4

To turn the omelette over, loosen the edges and slide it on to a large plate. Place the frying pan upside down over the omelette and, holding both tightly, carefully invert pan and plate. Cook the omelette for a further 2–3 minutes. Slide the omelette on to a serving plate and serve hot or at room temperature, garnished with parsley.

Omelette with Herbs

Sometimes the simplest dishes are the most satisfying. Fresh farm eggs, lightly soured cream and herbs make a speedy but superb meal.

INGREDIENTS

2 eggs
15 g / ½ oz / 1 tbsp butter
15 ml / 1 tbsp crème fraîche or soured cream
5 ml / 1 tsp chopped fresh mixed herbs (such as tarragon, chives, parsley or marjoram)
salt and freshly ground black pepper

Serves 1

VARIATIONS

Other omelette fillings could include sautéed sliced mushrooms, diced ham or crumbled crisp bacon, creamed spinach or thick tomato sauce and grated cheese.

1

Beat the eggs and salt and pepper in a bowl. Melt the butter in an omelette pan until foamy, then pour in the eggs. When the mixture starts to set on the base of the pan, lift up the sides with a palette knife and tilt the pan to allow the uncooked egg to run underneath.

2

When the omelette is set, but still soft on top, spoon the crème fraîche or soured cream over the centre and sprinkle with the herbs. Hold the pan over a warmed plate. With a palette knife, lift one edge of the omelette and fold it over the middle. Tilt the pan so that the omelette folds in thirds and slide it out on to the plate.

Egg-stuffed Tomatoes

Effective, but surprisingly easy to prepare, this is the perfect dish for a quick lunch. For the most enjoyable result, eat immediately.

INGREDIENTS

175 ml / 6 fl oz / ¾ cup mayonnaise
30 ml / 2 tbsp snipped fresh chives
30 ml / 2 tbsp torn fresh basil leaves
30 ml / 2 tbsp chopped fresh parsley
4 ripe tomatoes
4 hard-boiled eggs, sliced
salt
lettuce leaves, to serve

Serves 4

1

Mix the mayonnaise and herbs in a small bowl and set aside. Place the tomatoes core-end down and make deep cuts to within 1 cm / ½ in of the base. (There should be the same number of cuts in each tomato as there are slices of egg.)

2

Fan open the tomatoes and sprinkle with salt, then insert an egg slice into each slit. Place each stuffed tomato on a plate with lettuce leaves and serve with the herb mayonnaise.

Baked Cheese Polenta with Tomato Sauce

Polenta, or cornmeal, is a staple food in Italy. Cooked, cut into shapes when set, then baked with a tomato sauce, it makes a delicious meal.

1 litre / 1¾ pints / 4 cups water
5 ml / 1 tsp salt
250 g / 9 oz / 2¼ cups quick-cook polenta
5 ml / 1 tsp paprika
½ tsp grated nutmeg
30 ml / 2 tbsp olive oil
1 large onion, finely chopped
2 garlic cloves, crushed
900 g / 2 lb tomatoes, skinned and chopped or 2 x 400 g / 14 oz cans chopped tomatoes
15 ml / 1 tbsp tomato purée
5 ml / 1 tsp granulated sugar
75 g / 3 oz Gruyère cheese, grated salt and freshly ground black pepper

Serves 4

1

Preheat the oven to 200°C / 400°F / Gas Mark 6. Line a 28 x 18 cm / 11 x 7 in baking tin with clear film. Bring the water to the boil with the salt, pour in the polenta in a steady stream and cook, stirring constantly for 5 minutes or until it forms a thick mass. Beat in the paprika and nutmeg, then pour into the prepared tin and smooth the surface. Leave to cool and set.

2

Heat the oil in a large, shallow pan and cook the onion and garlic until soft. Stir in the tomatoes, tomato purée and sugar, with salt and pepper to taste. Bring to the boil, lower the heat and simmer for 20 minutes.

3

Turn out the polenta on to a chopping board, and cut into 5 cm / 2 in squares. Place half the squares in a greased baking dish. Spoon over half the tomato sauce, and sprinkle with half the cheese. Repeat the layers. Bake for about 25 minutes, until a golden colour.

Tortellini with Cream, Butter and Cheese

Pasta provides the perfect quick meal. The cream sauce takes only minutes to prepare, and tastes wonderful.

INGREDIENTS

450 g / 1 lb / 4 cups fresh tortellini
50 g / 2 oz / ¼ cup butter, plus extra
for greasing
300 ml / ½ pint / 1¼ cups double cream
115 g / 4 oz piece fresh Parmesan cheese
freshly grated nutmeg
salt and freshly ground black pepper
fresh herbs, to garnish

Serves 4–6

NOTE
Ring the changes with different cheeses, but don't try to use single cream because it will curdle.

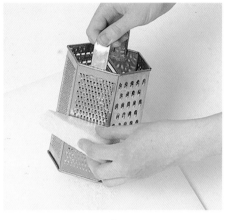

3

Grate the Parmesan and stir 75 g / 3 oz / ¾ cup into the sauce until melted. Season the sauce with salt, pepper and nutmeg. Preheat the grill.

4

Drain the pasta and spoon it into the serving dish. Pour over the sauce, sprinkle over the remaining cheese and grill until brown. Garnish and serve immediately.

1

Cook the pasta in a large saucepan of boiling salted water according to the manufacturer's instructions. Butter a flameproof serving dish.

2

Meanwhile, melt the butter in a medium saucepan and stir in the cream. Bring to the boil and cook for 2–3 minutes until slightly thickened.

Cauliflower Cheese

An old favourite that never loses its popularity, this is equally good with broccoli. Serve it with grilled locally-cured bacon for a special treat.

INGREDIENTS

450 g / 1 lb cauliflower, broken into florets
40 g / 1½ oz / 3 tbsp butter
40 g / 1½ oz / 6 tbsp plain flour
350 ml / 12 fl oz / 1½ cups milk
1 bay leaf
pinch of grated nutmeg
15 ml / 1 tbsp Dijon mustard
175 g / 6 oz / 1½ cups grated Gruyère or Emmenthal cheese
salt and freshly ground black pepper

Serves 4–6

1

Preheat the oven to 180°C / 350°F / Gas Mark 4. Lightly butter a large gratin dish or shallow baking dish.

2

Bring a large saucepan of salted water to the boil, add the cauliflower florets and cook for 6–8 minutes until just tender.

3

Melt the butter in a heavy saucepan over a medium heat, add the flour and cook until just golden, stirring occasionally. Gradually add the milk, stirring constantly until the sauce boils and thickens. Add the bay leaf and salt, pepper and nutmeg. Add the mustard. Reduce the heat and simmer for 5 minutes, stirring occasionally, then remove the bay leaf. Stir in half the cheese.

4

Arrange the cauliflower in the dish. Pour over the cheese sauce and sprinkle with the remaining cheese. Bake for about 20 minutes until bubbly and well browned.

Poached Eggs with Spinach

When the vegetable garden yields fresh spinach, serve this simple dish.

INGREDIENTS

25 g / 1 oz / 2 tbsp butter
450 g / 1 lb young spinach leaves
¹⁄₂ tsp vinegar
4 eggs
salt and freshly ground black pepper

For the hollandaise sauce
2 egg yolks
15 ml / 1 tbsp lemon juice
15 ml / 1 tbsp water
175 g / 6 oz / ³⁄₄ cup butter, diced
salt and white pepper

Serves 4

NOTE
For a well-shaped poached egg, swirl the water whirlpool-fashion before slipping the egg into the centre.

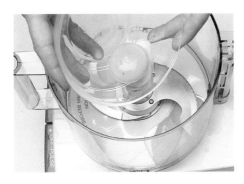

1

Make the hollandaise sauce. Whizz the egg yolks, lemon juice and water in a food processor. Melt the butter in a small pan until foaming. With the machine running, slowly pour the hot butter into the processor in a thin stream. Season the thickened sauce with more lemon juice if needed and salt and pepper. Transfer the sauce to a bowl, cover and keep warm.

2

Melt the butter in a heavy-based frying pan over a medium heat. Add the spinach and cook until wilted, stirring occasionally. Season and keep warm.

3

Bring a pan of lightly salted water to the boil and add the vinegar. Break an egg into a saucer and slide the egg into the water. Reduce the heat and simmer for a few minutes until the white is set and the yolk is still soft. Remove with a slotted spoon and drain. Trim any untidy edges with scissors and keep the poached egg warm. Poach the remaining eggs in the same way.

4

To serve, spoon the spinach on to warmed plates and make a hollow in each mound. Place the eggs on top and pour over a little hollandaise sauce.

Eggs in Pepper Nests

Pepper strips look pretty and provide an interesting base for baked eggs topped with cream.

INGREDIENTS

2 red peppers
1 green pepper
30 ml / 2 tbsp olive oil
1 large onion, finely sliced
2 garlic cloves, crushed
5–6 tomatoes, skinned and chopped
120 ml / 4 fl oz / ½ cup passata or
tomato juice
good pinch of dried basil
4 eggs
40 ml / 8 tsp single cream
pinch of cayenne pepper (optional)
salt and freshly ground black pepper

Serves 4

1

Preheat the oven to 180°C / 350°F / Gas Mark 4. Seed and thinly slice the peppers. Heat the olive oil in a large frying pan. Fry the onion and garlic gently for about 5 minutes, stirring, until softened.

2

Add the peppers to the onion and fry for 10 minutes. Stir in the tomatoes and passata or juice, the basil and seasoning. Cook gently for 10 minutes more until the peppers are soft.

3

Spoon the mixture into four ovenproof dishes. Make a hole in the centre of each and break in an egg. Spoon 10 ml / 2 tsp cream over the yolk of each egg and sprinkle with a little black pepper or cayenne. Bake for 12–15 minutes until the white of the egg is lightly set. Serve at once with crusty bread.

Eggs Baked in Ham and Potato Hash

INGREDIENTS

50 g / 2 oz / ¼ cup butter
1 large onion, chopped
350 g / 12 oz cooked ham, diced
450 g / 1 lb cooked potatoes, diced
115 g / 4 oz / 1 cup grated Cheddar cheese
30 ml / 2 tbsp tomato ketchup
30 ml / 2 tbsp Worcestershire sauce
6 eggs
few drops of Tabasco sauce
salt and freshly ground black pepper
chopped fresh chives, to garnish

Serves 6

___3___

Make six hollows in the hash. Break each egg in turn into a small bowl or saucer and slip into one of the hollows.

___4___

Melt the remaining butter. Season with Tabasco sauce, then dribble the seasoned butter over the eggs and hash. Bake for 15–20 minutes or until the eggs are set. Garnish with chives and serve.

___1___

Preheat the oven to 160°C / 325°F / Gas Mark 3. Melt half the butter in a frying pan. Cook the onion until soft, stirring occasionally, then tip it into a bowl and stir in the ham, potatoes, cheese, ketchup and Worcestershire sauce.

___2___

Season the mixture and spread it in a buttered baking dish in a layer about 2.5 cm / 1 in deep. Bake for 10 minutes.

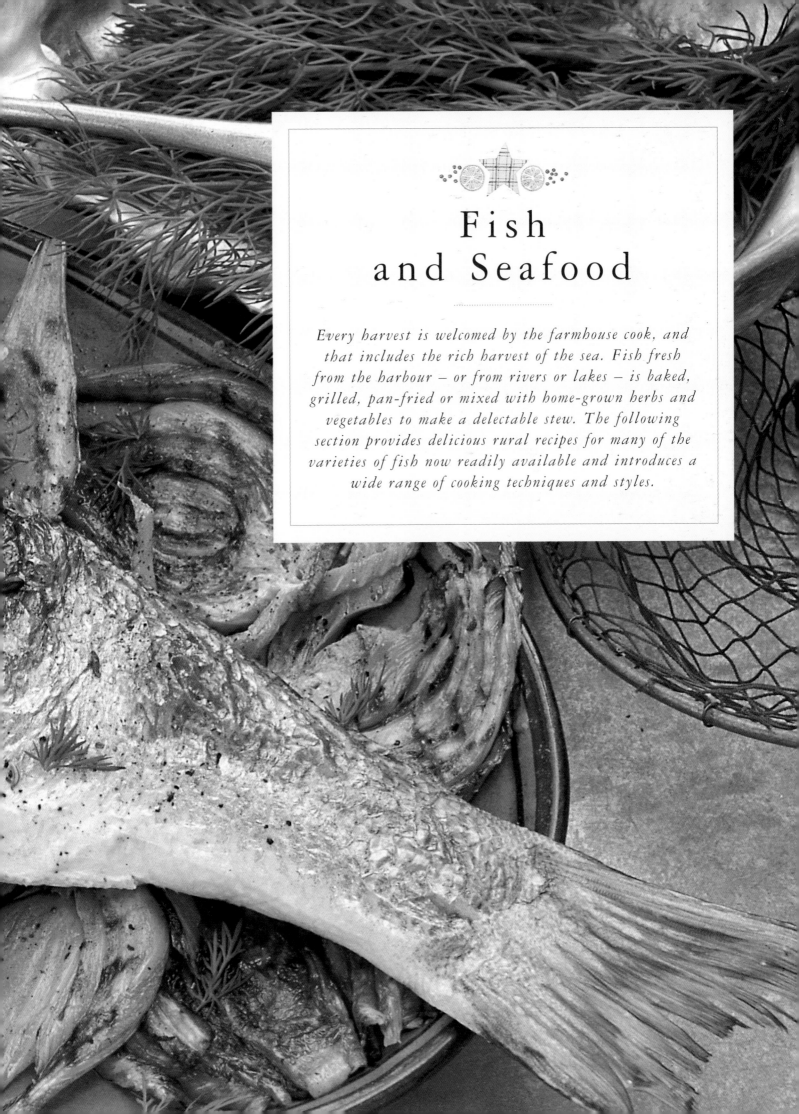

Fish
and Seafood

Every harvest is welcomed by the farmhouse cook, and that includes the rich harvest of the sea. Fish fresh from the harbour – or from rivers or lakes – is baked, grilled, pan-fried or mixed with home-grown herbs and vegetables to make a delectable stew. The following section provides delicious rural recipes for many of the varieties of fish now readily available and introduces a wide range of cooking techniques and styles.

Mackerel with Roasted Blueberries

Fresh blueberries burst with flavour when roasted, and their sharpness complements the rich flesh of mackerel very well.

INGREDIENTS

15 g / ½ oz / 2 tsp plain flour
4 small cooked, smoked mackerel fillets
50 g / 2 oz / 4 tbsp unsalted butter
juice of ½ lemon
salt and freshly ground black pepper

For the roasted blueberries
450 g / 1 lb blueberries
25 g / 1 oz / 2 tbsp caster sugar
15 g / ½ oz / 1 tbsp unsalted butter
salt and freshly ground black pepper

Serves 4

1

Preheat the oven to 200°C / 400°F / Gas Mark 6. Season the flour. Dip each fish fillet into the flour to coat it well.

2

Dot the butter on the fillets and bake in the oven for 20 minutes.

3

Place the blueberries, sugar, butter and seasoning in a separate small roasting tin and roast them, basting them occasionally, for 15 minutes. To serve, drizzle the lemon juice over the roasted mackerel, accompanied by the roasted blueberries.

Chunky Seafood Stew

There's no more pleasant way of spending an evening than sitting around the scrubbed farmhouse table and tucking into an excellent seafood stew.

INGREDIENTS

45 ml / 3 tbsp olive oil
2 large onions, chopped
1 small green pepper, seeded and sliced
3 carrots, chopped
3 garlic cloves, crushed
30 ml / 2 tbsp tomato purée
2 x 400 g / 14 oz cans chopped tomatoes
45 ml / 3 tbsp chopped fresh parsley
5 ml / 1 tsp chopped fresh thyme
15 ml / 1 tbsp shredded fresh basil
leaves
120 ml / 4 fl oz / ½ cup dry white wine
450 g / 1 lb raw prawns, peeled and
deveined, or cooked peeled prawns
1.5 kg / 3–3½ lb mussels or clams
(in shells), or a mixture, thoroughly
cleaned
900 g / 2 lb halibut or other firm,
white fish fillets, cut in 5 cm / 2 in
chunks
350 ml / 12 fl oz / 1½ cups fish stock
or water
salt and freshly ground black pepper
extra chopped fresh herbs, to garnish

Serves 6

2

Stir in the tomato purée, canned tomatoes, herbs and wine. Bring to the boil, lower the heat and simmer for 20 minutes. Add the prawns, mussels and/or clams, fish pieces and stock or water. Season with salt and pepper to taste.

3

Bring back to the boil, then simmer for 5–6 minutes, until the prawns turn pink, the fish flakes easily and the mussels and clams open. If using cooked prawns, add them for the last 2 minutes only. Serve in large soup plates, garnished with chopped herbs.

1

Heat the oil in a flameproof casserole. Add the onions, green pepper, carrots and garlic and cook for about 5 minutes, until tender.

Cod, Basil and Tomato with a Potato Thatch

With a green salad, this makes an ideal dish for lunch or a family supper.

INGREDIENTS

1 kg / 2 lb smoked cod
1 kg / 2 lb white cod
600 ml / 1 pint milk
2 sprigs basil
1 sprig lemon thyme
75 g / 3 oz butter
1 onion, peeled and chopped
75 g / 3 oz flour
30 ml / 2 tbsp tomato purée
2 tbsp chopped basil
12 medium-sized old potatoes
50 g / 2 oz butter
300 ml / ½ pint milk
salt and pepper
1 tbsp chopped parsley

Serves 8

1

Place both kinds of fish in a roasting pan with the milk, 1.2 litres/2 pints water and herbs. Simmer for about 3–4 minutes. Leave to cool in the liquid for about 20 minutes. Drain the fish, reserving the liquid for use in the sauce. Flake the fish, taking care to remove any skin and bone, which should be discarded.

2

Melt the butter in a pan, add the onion and cook for about 4 minutes until tender but not browned. Add the flour, tomato purée and half the basil. Gradually add the reserved fish stock, adding a little more milk if necessary to make a fairly thin sauce. Bring this to the boil, season with salt and pepper, and add the remaining basil. Add the fish carefully and stir gently. Pour into an ovenproof dish.

3

Preheat the oven to 180°C/350°F/Gas Mark 4. Boil the potatoes until tender. Add the butter and milk, and mash well. Add salt and pepper to taste and cover the fish, forking to create a pattern. If you like, you can freeze the pie at this stage. Bake for 30 minutes. Serve with chopped parsley.

Grilled Sea Bass with Fennel

Fennel has an unmistakable flavour, and goes particularly well with fish.

INGREDIENTS

*1 sea bass, 1.75 kg / 4–4½ lb,
cleaned
60–90 ml / 4–6 tbsp olive oil
10–15 ml / 2–3 tsp fennel seeds
2 large fennel bulbs, with fronds
attached
60 ml / 4 tbsp Pernod
salt and freshly ground black pepper*

Serves 6–8

1

With a sharp knife, make three or four deep cuts in both sides of the fish. Brush the fish with olive oil and season with salt and pepper. Sprinkle the fennel seeds in the stomach cavity and in the cuts. Set aside while you cook the fennel.

2

Preheat the grill. Trim the fennel fronds and quarter the bulbs lengthways. Remove the core and slice thinly. Reserve the fennel fronds. Put the fennel slices on the grill rack and brush with oil. Grill for 4 minutes on each side until tender. Transfer to a large dish or platter.

3

Place the fish on the oiled grill rack and position about 13 cm / 5 in from the heat. Grill for 10–12 minutes on each side, brushing occasionally with oil. Transfer the fish to the platter on top of the fennel. Garnish with the fennel fronds. Heat the Pernod in a small pan, light it and pour it, flaming, over the fish. Serve at once.

Herbed Halibut Mille-feuille

The herbs add their own special flavours to the creamy fish.

INGREDIENTS

250 g / 9 oz puff pastry
butter for baking sheet
1 egg, beaten
1 small onion
1 tbsp fresh ginger, grated
7 ml / ½ tbsp oil
150 ml / ¼ pint / ⅔ cup fish stock
15 ml / 1 tbsp dry sherry
350 g / 12 oz halibut, cooked and
flaked
225 g / 8 oz crab meat
salt and pepper
1 avocado
juice of 1 lime
1 mango
1 tbsp chopped mixed parsley, thyme
and chives, to garnish

Serves 2

1

Roll the pastry out into a square
25 × 25 cm / 10 × 10 in, trim the edges
and place on a buttered baking sheet. Prick
with a fork, then rest it in the refrigerator
for at least 30 minutes. Preheat the oven to
230°C / 450°F / Gas Mark 8. Brush the
top with beaten egg, and bake for
10–15 minutes or until golden.

3

Fry the onion and ginger in the oil until
tender. Add the fish stock and sherry, and
simmer for 5 minutes. Add the halibut and
crab meat, and season to taste. Peel and
chop the avocado and toss in the lime
juice. Peel and chop the mango reserving a
few slices for garnishing. Add the avocado
and the mango to the fish.

2

Let the pastry cool for a few minutes, then
cut it twice across in one direction and
once in the other to make six pieces. Leave
to cool completely.

4

Build up alternate layers of fish and pastry,
starting and finishing with a piece of pastry.
Serve garnished with herbs and mango slices.

Salmon and Ginger Pie

This exceptional pie is highly
recommended. This recipe uses
salmon's special flavour to the full.

INGREDIENTS

800 g / 1¾ lb middle cut of salmon
45 ml / 3 tbsp walnut oil
15 ml / 1 tbsp lime juice
2 tsp chopped fresh lemon thyme
30 ml / 2 tbsp white wine
salt and pepper
40 0g / 14 oz puff pastry
50 g / 2 oz / ½ cup flaked almonds
3–4 pieces stem ginger in syrup,
chopped

Serves 4–6

1

Split the salmon in half, remove all the
bones and skin and divide into 4 fillets.
Mix the oil, lime juice, thyme, wine and
pepper, and pour over the fish. Leave to
marinate overnight in the refrigerator.

2

Divide the pastry into 2 pieces, one slightly
larger than the other, and roll out – the
smaller piece should be large enough to take
2 of the salmon fillets and the second piece
about 5 cm / 2 in larger all round.

3

Drain the fillets. Discard the marinade.
Preheat the oven to 190°C / 375°F / Gas
Mark 5. Place 2 of the fillets on the smaller
piece of pastry, and season. Add the
almonds and ginger and cover with the
other 2 fillets.

4

Season again, cover with the second piece
of pastry and seal well. Brush with beaten
egg and decorate with any leftover pastry.
Bake for 40 minutes.

Leek and Monkfish with Thyme Sauce

Monkfish is a well-known fish now, thanks to its excellent flavour and firm texture.

INGREDIENTS

1 kg / 2 lb monkfish, cubed
salt and pepper
75 g / 3 oz / generous ⅓ cup butter
4 leeks, sliced
1 tbsp flour
150 ml / ¼ pint / ⅔ cup fish or
vegetable stock
2 tsp finely chopped fresh thyme,
plus more to garnish
juice of 1 lemon
150 ml / ¼ pint / ⅔ cup single cream
radicchio, to garnish

Serves 4

1

Season the fish to taste. Melt about a third of the butter in a pan, and fry the fish for a short time. Put to one side.

2

Fry the leeks in the pan with another third of the butter until they have softened. Put these to one side with the fish.

3

In a saucepan, melt the rest of the butter, add the butter from the pan, stir in the flour, and add the stock. As the sauce thickens, add the thyme and lemon juice.

4

Return the leeks and monkfish to the pan and cook gently for a few minutes. Add the cream and season to taste. Serve immediately garnished with thyme and radicchio leaves.

Fish Stew with Calvados, Parsley and Dill

This rustic stew harbours all sorts of interesting flavours and will please and intrigue.
Many varieties of fish can be used, just choose the freshest and best.

INGREDIENTS

1 kg / 2 lb assorted white fish
1 tbsp chopped parsley, plus a few
leaves to garnish
225 g / 8 oz mushrooms
225 g / 8 oz can of tomatoes
salt and pepper
2 tsp flour
15 g / ½ oz / 1 tbsp butter
450 ml / ¾ pint cider
45 ml / 3 tbsp Calvados
1 large bunch fresh dill sprigs,
reserving 4 fronds to garnish

Serves 4

1

Chop the fish roughly and place it in a casserole or stewing pot with the parsley, mushrooms and tomatoes, adding salt and pepper to taste.

2

Preheat the oven to 180°C/350°F/Gas Mark 4. Work the flour into the butter. Heat the cider and stir in the flour and butter mixture a little at a time. Cook, stirring, until it has thickened slightly.

3

Add the cider mixture and the remaining ingredients to the fish and mix gently. Cover and bake for about 30 minutes. Serve garnished with sprigs of dill and parsley leaves.

Griddled Trout with Bacon

This dish can also be cooked on the barbecue.

INGREDIENTS

25 g / 1 oz / 1 tbsp plain flour
4 trout, cleaned and gutted
75 g / 3 oz streaky bacon
50 g / 2 oz / 4 tbsp butter
15 ml / 1 tbsp olive oil
juice of ½ lemon
salt and freshly ground
black pepper

Serves 4

1

Pat the trout dry with kitchen roll and
mix the flour and seasoning together.

2

Roll the trout in the seasoned flour mixture
and wrap tightly in the streaky bacon.
Heat a heavy frying pan. Heat the butter and
oil in the pan and fry the trout for 5 minutes
on each side. Serve immediately, with the
lemon juice drizzled on top.

Trout Fillets with Spinach and Mushroom Sauce

Field mushrooms form the basis of this rich sauce, served with trout that has been filleted to make it easier to eat.

INGREDIENTS

4 brown or rainbow trout, filleted and skinned to make 8 fillets

For the spinach and mushroom sauce
75 g / 3 oz / 6 tbsp butter
¼ medium onion, chopped
225 g / 8 oz closed field mushrooms, chopped
300 ml / ½ pint / 1¼ cups boiling chicken stock
225 g / 8 oz frozen chopped spinach
10 ml / 2 tsp cornflour, mixed to a paste with 15 ml / 1 tbsp cold water
150 ml / ¼ pint / ⅔ cup crème fraîche grated nutmeg
salt and freshly ground black pepper

Serves 4

NOTE
Spinach and mushroom sauce is also good with fillets of cod, haddock and sole.

2

Stir the cornflour paste into the mushroom mixture. Bring to the boil, then simmer gently to thicken. Purée the mixture. Add the crème fraîche and season with salt, pepper and nutmeg. Blend briefly, then scrape into a serving jug and keep warm.

3

Melt the remaining butter in a large non-stick frying pan. Season the trout and cook for 6 minutes, turning once. Serve with the sauce either poured over or served separately. New potatoes and baby corn would be ideal accompaniments.

1

To make the sauce, melt two-thirds of the butter in a frying pan and fry the onion until soft. Add the mushrooms and cook until the juices begin to run. Stir in the stock and the spinach and cook until the spinach has thawed completely.

Trout with Almonds

This quick and easy recipe can be cooked for four, adapted by cooking the trout in two frying pans or in batches.

INGREDIENTS

*2 trout, about 350 g / 12 oz each,
cleaned
40 g / 1½ oz / 6 tbsp plain flour
50 g / 2 oz / ¼ cup butter
25 g / 1 oz / ¼ cup flaked or sliced
almonds
30 ml / 2 tbsp dry white wine
salt and freshly ground black pepper*

Serves 2

NOTE

The easiest way to coat the trout is to put the flour in a large polythene bag and season with salt and pepper. Place the trout, one at a time, in the bag and shake until evenly coated. Shake off the excess flour from the fish.

1

Coat the trout in the flour, seasoned with salt and pepper. Melt half the butter in a large frying pan. When it is foamy, add the trout and cook for 6–7 minutes on each side, until the skin is golden brown and the flesh next to the bone is opaque. Transfer the fish to warmed plates and keep hot.

2

Add the remaining butter to the pan and cook the almonds until just lightly browned. Add the wine to the pan and boil for 1 minute, stirring constantly, until slightly syrupy. Pour or spoon over the fish and serve at once.

Tuna with Garlic, Tomatoes and Herbs

In France, where this recipe originated, dried wild herbs are used, but fresh herbs are fine.

INGREDIENTS

*4 tuna steaks, about 2.5 cm / 1 in
thick (175–200 g / 6–7 oz each)
30–45 ml / 2–3 tbsp olive oil
3–4 garlic cloves, finely chopped
60 ml / 4 tbsp dry white wine
3 ripe tomatoes, skinned, seeded and
chopped
15–30 ml / 1–2 tbsp dried mixed
herbs
salt and freshly ground black pepper
fresh basil leaves, to garnish*

Serves 4

NOTE

Tuna is often served pink in the middle. If you prefer it cooked through, reduce the heat and cook for a few extra minutes.

1

Season the tuna steaks with salt and pepper. Set a heavy-based frying pan over a high heat. When very hot, add the oil and swirl to coat. Add the tuna steaks and press down gently, then reduce the heat to medium and cook for 6–8 minutes, turning once, until just slightly pink in the centre.

2

Transfer the steaks to a serving plate and keep hot. Add the garlic to the pan and fry for 15–20 seconds, then pour in the wine and boil until reduced by half. Add the tomatoes and herbs and cook for 2–3 minutes. Season with pepper and pour over the fish steaks. Serve, garnished with fresh basil leaves.

Pan-fried Garlic Sardines

Lightly fry a sliced clove of garlic to garnish the fish. This dish could also be made with sprats or fresh anchovies if available.

INGREDIENTS

8 fresh sardines
30 ml / 2 tbsp olive oil
4 garlic cloves
finely grated rind of 2 lemons
30 ml / 2 tbsp chopped fresh parsley
salt and freshly ground black pepper

For the tomato bread
2 large ripe beefsteak tomatoes
8 slices crusty bread, toasted

Serves 4

1

Gut and clean the sardines. Pat them dry with kitchen paper.

2

Heat the oil in a frying pan and cook the garlic cloves until soft.

3

Remove the garlic from the pan, then fry the sardines for 4–5 minutes. Sprinkle over the lemon rind, parsley and seasoning.

4

Cut the tomatoes in half and rub them on to the toast. Discard the skins. Serve each sardine on a slice of the tomato toast.

Stuffed Sardines

Adding a savoury sultana and pine nut stuffing takes sardines into a more sophisticated league.

8 fresh sardines
30 ml / 2 tbsp olive oil
75 g / 3 oz / 1½ cups breadcrumbs
50 g / 2 oz / ⅓ cup sultanas
50 g / 2 oz / ⅔ cup pine nuts
50 g / 2 oz can anchovy fillets, drained
60 ml / 4 tbsp chopped fresh parsley
1 onion, finely chopped
salt and freshly ground black pepper
lemon wedges, to garnish

Serves 4

___
3

Stuff each sardine with the mixture. Close
the fish firmly and closely pack together in
a single layer in an ovenproof dish.

___
4

Scatter any remaining filling over the
sardines and drizzle with olive oil. Bake for
30 minutes and serve with lemon wedges.

___
1

Preheat the oven to 200°C / 400°F / Gas
Mark 6. Gut and clean the sardines; dry
with kitchen paper. Heat the oil in a frying
pan and fry the breadcrumbs until golden.

___
2

Add the sultanas, pine nuts, anchovies,
parsley, onion and seasoning to the
breadcrumbs.

Poached Cod, Greek-style

Cod is often served with little preparation. Although it can be delicious in its simplest form, it sometimes deserves more sophisticated treatment. This recipe is a little more involved, poaching the fish with onions and tomatoes.

INGREDIENTS

300 ml / ½ pint / 1¼ cups olive oil
2 onions, thinly sliced
3 large well-flavoured tomatoes, roughly chopped
3 garlic cloves, thinly sliced
5 ml / 1 tsp granulated sugar
5 ml / 1 tsp chopped fresh dill
5 ml / 1 tsp chopped fresh mint
5 ml / 1 tsp chopped fresh celery leaves
15 ml / 1 tbsp chopped fresh parsley
300 ml / ½ pint / 1¼ cups water
6 cod steaks
juice of 1 lemon
salt and freshly ground black pepper
extra dill, mint or parsley, to garnish

Serves 6

1

Heat the oil in a large, shallow pan and cook the onions until pale golden. Stir in the tomatoes, garlic, sugar, dill, mint, celery leaves and parsley. Pour over the water. Season with salt and pepper, then simmer, uncovered, for 25 minutes, until the liquid has reduced by one-third.

2

Add the cod steaks and cook gently for 10–12 minutes, until the fish is just cooked. Remove from the heat and pour over the lemon juice. Cover and leave to stand for about 20 minutes before serving. Arrange the cod in a dish and spoon the sauce over the top. Garnish with herbs and serve warm or cold.

Cod with Lentils and Leeks

This unusual dish is great for entertaining. The vegetables can be cooked ahead of time and the fish baked while the first course is served.

INGREDIENTS

150 g / 5 oz / scant 1 cup green lentils, rinsed
1 bay leaf
1 garlic clove, finely chopped
grated rind of 1 orange
grated rind of 1 lemon
pinch of ground cumin
15 g / ½ oz / 1 tbsp butter
450 g / 1 lb leeks, thinly sliced
300 ml / ½ pint / 1¼ cups whipping cream
15 ml / 1 tbsp lemon juice, or to taste
800 g / 1¾ lb thick cod or haddock fillets, skinned
salt and freshly ground black pepper

Serves 4

1

Put the lentils, bay leaf and garlic in a large saucepan and enough water to cover by 5 cm / 2 in. Bring to the boil, boil gently for 10 minutes, then reduce the heat and simmer for 15–30 minutes more, until the lentils are just tender.

2

Drain the lentils and discard the bay leaf, then stir in half the orange rind and all the lemon rind. Season with the ground cumin and salt and pepper. Transfer to a shallow baking dish or gratin dish. Preheat the oven to 190°C / 375°F / Gas Mark 5.

3

Melt the butter over a medium heat in a saucepan, add the leeks and cook gently, stirring frequently, until just softened. Add 250 ml / 8 fl oz / 1 cup of the cream and the remaining orange rind and cook gently for 15–20 minutes until the leeks have softened completely and the cream has thickened slightly. Stir in the lemon juice and season with salt and plenty of pepper.

4

Cut the fish into four pieces and remove any remaining bones. Season the fish with salt and pepper, place the pieces on top of the lentil mixture and press down slightly. Cover each piece of fish with a quarter of the leek mixture and divide the remaining cream between them. Bake for about 30 minutes until the fish is cooked thoroughly and the topping is golden.

Special Seafood Stew

Not all farmhouse cooking is plain and pastoral — on high days and holidays family and friends will celebrate with a special dish, like this classic seafood stew from Spain.

INGREDIENTS

1 cooked lobster
24 fresh mussels
1 large monkfish tail
15 ml / 1 tbsp plain flour
225 g / 8 oz squid rings
90 ml / 6 tbsp olive oil
12 large raw prawns

450 g / 1 lb ripe tomatoes
2 large mild onions
4 garlic cloves, crushed
30 ml / 2 tbsp brandy
2 bay leaves
5 ml / 1 tsp paprika
1 red chilli, seeded and chopped

300 ml / ½ pint / 1¼ cups fish stock
15 g / ½ oz / 3 tbsp ground almonds
30 ml / 2 tbsp chopped fresh parsley
salt and freshly ground black pepper

Serves 6

1

Cut the lobster in half and remove the dark intestine that runs down the length of the tail. Crack the claws using a hammer. Scrub the mussels, discarding any that are damaged and any open ones that do not close when tapped with a knife. Cut the monkfish fillets away from the central cartilage and cut each fillet into three.

2

Season the flour and toss the monkfish and squid in it. Heat the oil in a frying pan. Add the monkfish and squid and fry quickly; remove from the pan. Fry the prawns, then remove from the pan. Plunge the tomatoes into boiling water for 30 seconds, then refresh in cold water. Peel away the skins and chop roughly.

3

Chop the onions and add to the pan with two-thirds of the garlic. Fry for 3 minutes, then add the brandy and ignite with a taper. When the flames die down, add the tomatoes, bay leaves, paprika, chilli and stock. Bring to the boil, reduce the heat and simmer for 5 minutes.

4

Add the mussels, cover and cook for 3–4 minutes, until the shells have opened. Remove the mussels from the sauce and discard any that remain closed. Arrange all the fish, including the lobster, in a large flameproof serving dish.

5

Blend the ground almonds to a paste with the remaining garlic and parsley and stir into the sauce. Season with salt and pepper. Pour the sauce over the fish and lobster and cook gently for about 5 minutes until hot. Serve immediately with a green salad and plenty of warmed bread.

Seafood Risotto

Risotto is the perfect example of a rustic dish that can be adapted to take advantage of whatever is in season. This seafood version varies, depending on the current catch.

INGREDIENTS

*60 ml / 4 tbsp sunflower oil
1 onion, chopped
2 garlic cloves, crushed
225 g / 8 oz / generous 1 cup arborio rice
105 ml / 7 tbsp white wine
1.5 litres / 2½ pints / 6 cups hot fish stock
350 g / 12 oz mixed seafood, such as raw prawns, mussels, squid rings or clams, prepared according to type
grated rind of ½ lemon
30 ml / 2 tbsp tomato purée
15 ml / 1 tbsp chopped fresh parsley
salt and freshly ground black pepper*

Serves 4

1

Heat the oil in a heavy-based saucepan and fry the onion and garlic gently until soft. Add the rice and stir to coat the grains with oil. Pour in the wine and stir over a medium heat until it has been absorbed.

2

Ladle in 150 ml / ¼ pint / ⅔ cup of the hot stock and cook, stirring constantly, until the liquid is absorbed by the rice. Continue stirring and adding stock in similar quantities, until half is left. This should take about 10 minutes.

3

Stir in the seafood and cook for 2–3 minutes. Add the remaining stock as before, until the rice is cooked. It should be quite creamy and the grains just tender. Stir in the lemon rind, tomato purée and parsley. Season with salt and pepper and serve warm.

Italian Prawn Skewers

These are delicious, whether grilled or cooked on the barbecue, and would be ideal for a summer party.

INGREDIENTS

*900 g / 2 lb raw tiger prawns, peeled
60 ml / 4 tbsp olive oil
45 ml / 3 tbsp vegetable oil
175 g / 6 oz / 1¼ cups very fine dry breadcrumbs
1 garlic clove, crushed
15 ml / 1 tbsp chopped fresh parsley
salt and freshly ground black pepper
lemon wedges, to serve*

Serves 4

1

Slit the prawns down their backs and remove the dark veins. Rinse in cold water and pat dry. Mix the oils in a large bowl and add the prawns, turning them in the oil to coat evenly.

2

Add the breadcrumbs, garlic and parsley to the bowl, with salt and pepper to taste. Toss the oiled prawns in the mixture to coat them evenly. Cover and leave to marinate for 1 hour.

3

Preheat the grill. Thread the prawns on to four metal skewers, curling them up as you do so, so that the tail is skewered in the middle. Place the skewers in the grill pan and cook for about 2 minutes on each side, until the breadcrumbs are golden. Serve with lemon wedges.

Crab Cakes

These crab cakes are full of flavour thanks to mustard, horseradish and Worcestershire sauce.

INGREDIENTS

450 g / 1 lb fresh white crab meat
1 egg, well beaten
5 ml / 1 tsp Dijon mustard
10 ml / 2 tsp prepared horseradish
10 ml / 2 tsp Worcestershire sauce
8 spring onions, finely chopped
45 ml / 3 tbsp chopped fresh parsley
75 g / 3 oz / 1½ cups fresh breadcrumbs
15 ml / 1 tbsp whipping cream
(optional)
115 g / 4 oz / 1 cup dry breadcrumbs
40 g / 1½ oz / 3 tbsp butter
salt and freshly ground black pepper
lemon wedges and fresh dill sprigs, for
serving

Serves 3–6

1

In a mixing bowl, combine the crab meat, egg, mustard, horseradish, Worcestershire sauce, spring onions, parsley and fresh breadcrumbs. Mix gently, leaving the pieces of crab meat as large as possible. Season to taste. If the mixture is too dry to hold together, add the cream. Divide the crab mixture into six portions and shape into round, flat cakes.

2

Spread out the dry breadcrumbs on a plate. Coat the crab cakes on both sides. Melt the butter in a frying pan. Fry the crab cakes for about 3 minutes on each side or until golden. Add more fat if necessary. Serve with lemon wedges and dill.

Baked Stuffed Crab

Good cooking means meals that are good looking as well as tasty. This recipe scores on all counts.

INGREDIENTS

4 freshly cooked crabs
1 celery stick, diced
1 spring onion, finely chopped
1 small fresh green chilli, seeded and
finely chopped
75 ml / 5 tbsp mayonnaise
30 ml / 2 tbsp fresh lemon juice
15 ml / 1 tbsp snipped fresh chives
25 g / 1 oz / ½ cup fresh breadcrumbs
50 g / 2 oz / ½ cup grated Cheddar
cheese
25 g / 1 oz / 2 tbsp butter, melted
salt and freshly ground black pepper
fresh parsley sprigs, to garnish

Serves 4

1

Preheat the oven to 190°C / 375°F / Gas Mark 3. Remove the meat from the crab body and claws. Reserve the whole shells.

2

Scrub the crab shells. Cut open the seam on the underside with scissors. The inner part of the shell should break off cleanly along the seam. Rinse the shells and dry them well.

3

In a bowl, combine the crab meat, celery, spring onion, chilli, mayonnaise, lemon juice and chives. Season and mix. In a separate bowl, toss together the breadcrumbs, cheese and melted butter.

4

Pile the crab mixture into the shells. Sprinkle with the cheese mixture. Bake for about 20 minutes until golden brown. Serve hot, garnished with parsley.

Poultry
and Game

Chicken and duck play a prominent role in farmhouse cookery, with slow-cooked casseroles, hearty pies and handsome roasts filling the kitchen with tempting aromas. Game birds and venison are valued in their season, and country cooks know just how delicious rabbit can be. The following pages are full of delicious recipes that will be particularly enjoyed as the main meal of the day.

Traditional Chicken Pie

With its golden crust and rich chicken and vegetable filling, an old-fashioned chicken pie is a favourite family dish.

INGREDIENTS

50 g / 2 oz / 4 tbsp butter
1 onion, chopped
3 carrots, diced
1 parsnip, diced
20 g / ¾ oz / 3 tbsp plain flour
350 ml / 12 fl oz / 1½ cups chicken stock
75 ml / 5 tbsp medium sherry
75 ml / 5 tbsp dry white wine
175 ml / 6 fl oz / ¾ cup whipping cream
115 g / 4 oz / ¾ cup frozen peas, thawed
350 g / 12 oz cooked chicken meat, in chunks
5 ml / 1 tsp dried thyme

15 ml / 1 tbsp finely chopped fresh parsley
salt and freshly ground black pepper
1 egg, beaten with 30 ml / 2 tbsp milk, to glaze

For the pastry
175 g / 6 oz / 1½ cups plain flour
½ tsp salt
115 g / 4 oz / ½ cup lard or vegetable fat
30–45 ml / 2–3 tbsp iced water

Serves 6

1

For the pastry, sift the flour and salt into a mixing bowl. Rub in the fat until the mixture resembles coarse breadcrumbs, then add enough iced water to form a dough. Dust with flour, wrap and chill.

2

Preheat the oven to 200°C / 400°F / Gas Mark 6. Heat half the butter in a saucepan. Add the onion, carrots and parsnip and cook for 10 minutes, until softened. Remove from the pan with a slotted spoon.

3

Melt the remaining butter in the pan. Add the flour and cook for 2 minutes, stirring constantly. Stir in the stock, sherry and white wine. Bring the sauce to the boil, and cook for 1 minute, stirring constantly.

4

Stir the cream, peas, chicken, thyme and parsley into the sauce. Season to taste with salt and pepper. Simmer for 1 minute, stirring, then transfer the mixture to a 2 litre / 3½ pint / 8 cup pie dish.

5

Roll out the pastry. Cover the pie and trim off the excess pastry. Dampen the rim of the dish. With a fork, press the pastry to the rim to seal. Cut decorative shapes from the pastry trimmings. Brush the pastry all over with the egg glaze. Arrange the pastry shapes on top.

6

Brush again with the egg glaze. Make one or two holes in the crust so steam can escape during baking. Bake the pie for about 35 minutes, until the pastry is golden brown. Serve hot.

Chicken and Sweetcorn Stew

Americans would serve this rustic stew with biscuits, which resemble what the British call scones. The combination works remarkably well.

INGREDIENTS

1.75 kg / 4 lb chicken, cut in serving
pieces
paprika
30 ml / 2 tbsp olive oil
25 g / 1 oz / 2 tbsp butter
450 g / 1 lb onions, chopped
1 green or yellow pepper, cored, seeded
and chopped
400 g / 14 oz can chopped tomatoes
250 ml / 8 fl oz / 1 cup white wine
475 ml / 16 fl oz / 2 cups chicken
stock or water
45 ml / 3 tbsp chopped fresh parsley
½ tsp Tabasco sauce
15 ml / 1 tbsp Worcestershire sauce
275 g / 10 oz / 2 cups sweetcorn
kernels (fresh, frozen, or drained
canned)
150 g / 5 oz / 1 cup broad beans
(fresh or frozen)
20 g / ¾ oz / 3 tbsp plain flour
salt and freshly ground black pepper
flat leaf parsley sprigs, to garnish

Serves 6

1

Rinse the chicken pieces under cool water and pat dry with kitchen paper. Sprinkle each piece lightly with salt and paprika.

2

Heat the oil and butter in a large, heavy-based saucepan. Add the chicken pieces and fry until golden brown on all sides. Remove with tongs and set aside.

3

Reduce the heat to low and cook the onions and pepper for 8–10 minutes, until softened. Stir in the tomatoes, wine, stock or water, parsley and sauces. Turn up the heat and bring to the boil.

4

Return the chicken to the pan, pushing it down in the sauce. Cover, reduce the heat and simmer for 30 minutes, stirring occasionally.

5

Add the corn and beans and mix well. Partly cover and cook for 30 minutes more. Skim off or blot any surface fat.

6

Mix the flour with a little water to make a paste. Gradually add 175 ml / 6 fl oz / ¾ cup of the hot liquid from the pan. Stir this mixture into the stew and season with salt and pepper. Cook for 5–8 minutes more, stirring occasionally. Garnish and serve.

Chicken and Mushroom Cobbler

*There's something very homely about a cobbler, with its scone topping and satisfying filling.
Adding wild mushrooms enriches the flavour but button mushrooms are fine for a family meal.*

INGREDIENTS

*60 ml / 4 tbsp vegetable oil
1 onion, chopped
1 celery stick, sliced
1 small carrot, peeled and diced
3 skinless, boneless chicken breasts
450 g / 1 lb / 4 cups mixed field
mushrooms and wild mushrooms, sliced
40 g / 1½ oz / 6 tbsp plain flour
500 ml / 18 fl oz / 2¼ cups hot
chicken stock
10 ml / 2 tsp Dijon mustard
30 ml / 2 tbsp medium sherry
10 ml / 2 tsp wine vinegar
salt and freshly ground black pepper*

For the cobbler topping
*275 g / 10 oz / 2½ cups self-raising
flour
pinch of celery salt
pinch of cayenne pepper
115 g / 4 oz / ½ cup butter, diced
50 g / 2 oz / ½ cup grated Cheddar cheese
150 ml / ¼ pint / ⅔ cup cold water
1 beaten egg, to glaze*

Serves 4

1

Preheat the oven to 200°C / 400°F / Gas
Mark 6. Heat the oil in a large, heavy-
based saucepan and fry the onion, celery
and carrot gently for 8–10 minutes, to
soften without colouring. Cube the
chicken, then add to the pan and cook
briefly. Add the mushrooms, fry until the
juices run, then stir in the flour.

2

Remove the pan from the heat and
gradually stir in the stock. Return the pan
to the heat, and simmer gently to thicken,
stirring all the time. Stir in the mustard,
sherry, vinegar and seasoning.

3

To make the topping, sift the flour, celery
salt and cayenne into a bowl or food
processor fitted with a metal blade. Rub in
the butter and half the cheese until the
mixture resembles coarse breadcrumbs. Add
the water and combine without over-mixing.

4

Turn the dough on to a floured board, form
it into a round and flatten to a thickness of
about 1 cm / ½ in. Cut out as many 5 cm /
2 in shapes as you can, using a cutter.

5

Transfer the chicken mixture to a 1.2 litre /
2 pint / 5 cup pie dish, then overlap the
cobbler shapes around the edge. Brush with
beaten egg, scatter with the remaining
cheese and bake for 25–30 minutes until
the topping has risen well and is golden.

Chicken with Sloe Gin and Juniper

*Juniper is used in the manufacture of gin, and this dish is flavoured with both
sloe gin and juniper. Sloe gin is easy to make and
has a wonderful flavour, but it can also be bought ready-made.*

INGREDIENTS

2 tbsp butter
30 ml / 2 tbsp sunflower oil
8 chicken breast fillets, skinned
350 g / 12 oz carrots, cooked
1 clove garlic, peeled and crushed
1 tbsp finely chopped parsley
60 ml / 2 fl oz / ¼ cup chicken stock
60 ml / 2 fl oz / ¼ cup red wine
60 ml / 2 fl oz / ¼ cup sloe gin
1 tsp crushed juniper berries
salt and pepper
1 bunch basil, to garnish

Serves 8

1

Melt the butter with the oil in a pan, and
sauté the chicken fillets until they are
browned on all sides.

2

In a food processor, combine all the
remaining ingredients except the basil,
and blend to a smooth purée. If the
mixture seems too thick add a little more
red wine or water until a thinner
consistency is reached.

3

Put the chicken breasts in a pan, pour the
sauce over the top and cook until the
chicken is cooked through, which should
take about 15 minutes. Adjust the
seasoning and serve garnished with
chopped fresh basil leaves.

Turkey with Apples and Bay Leaves

*Apples from the orchard combine with bay leaves and Madeira to create
a delicious turkey casserole with a handsome garnish.*

INGREDIENTS

75 g / 3 oz / 6 tbsp butter
*675 g / 1½ lb turkey breast fillets,
cut into 2 cm / ¾ in slices*
4 tart cooking apples, peeled and sliced
3 bay leaves
90 ml / 6 tbsp Madeira
150 ml / ¼ pint / ⅔ cup chicken stock
10 ml / 2 tsp cornflour
150 ml / ¼ pint / ⅔ cup double cream
salt and freshly ground black pepper

Serves 4

1

Preheat the oven to 180°C / 350°F / Gas
Mark 4. Melt a third of the butter in a
large, shallow pan and fry the turkey breast
fillets until sealed on all sides. Transfer to a
casserole and add half the remaining butter
and half the apple slices and cook gently for
1–2 minutes.

2

Tuck the bay leaves around the turkey
breasts. Stir in 60 ml / 4 tbsp of the
Madeira and all the stock. Simmer for
3–4 minutes, then cover and bake for 40
minutes.

3

Mix the cornflour to a paste with a little of
the cream, then stir in the rest of the
cream. Add this mixture to the casserole,
season, stir well, then return to the oven for
10 minutes to allow the sauce to thicken.

4

To make the garnish, melt the remaining
butter in a frying pan and gently fry the
remaining apple slices until just tender.
Add the remaining Madeira and set it
alight. Once the flames have died down,
continue to cook the apple slices until they
are lightly browned. Arrange them on top
of the turkey mixture.

Roast Turkey with Mushroom Stuffing

A fresh farm turkey tastes wonderful with a wild mushroom stuffing.
Serve it with a wild mushroom gravy for maximum impact.

INGREDIENTS

5 kg / 11 lb free range turkey, dressed
weight
butter, for basting
watercress, to garnish

For the mushroom stuffing
50 g / 2 oz / 4 tbsp butter
1 onion, chopped
225 g / 8 oz wild mushrooms, chopped
75 g / 3 oz / 1½ cups fresh white
breadcrumbs
115 g / 4 oz pork sausages, skinned
1 small fresh truffle, sliced (optional)
5 drops truffle oil (optional)
salt and freshly ground black pepper

For the gravy
75 ml / 5 tbsp medium sherry
400 ml / 14 fl oz / 1⅔ cups chicken stock
20 ml / 4 tsp cornflour
5 ml / 1 tsp Dijon mustard
10 ml / 2 tsp water
½ tsp red wine vinegar

Serves 6–8

1

Preheat the oven to 220°C / 425°F / Gas Mark 7. To make the stuffing, melt the butter in a saucepan and fry the onion gently without colouring. Add the mushrooms and stir until their juices begin to flow. Transfer from the pan to a bowl and add all the remaining ingredients, including the truffle and truffle oil if using. Season and stir well to combine.

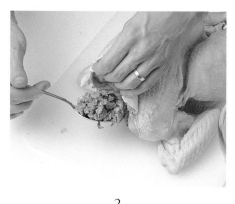

2

Spoon the stuffing into the neck cavity of the turkey and enclose, fastening the skin on the underside with a skewer.

3

Rub the skin of the turkey with butter, place in a large roasting tin and roast for 50 minutes. Lower the temperature to 180°C / 350°F / Gas Mark 4 and cook for 2½ hours more.

4

Transfer the turkey to a carving board, cover loosely with foil and keep hot. Spoon off the fat from the roasting juices, then place the tin over a medium heat until the juices are reduced to a sediment. Stir in the sherry and incorporate the sediment, then stir in the chicken stock.

5

Place the cornflour and mustard in a small bowl. Stir in the water and wine vinegar. Stir this mixture into the juices in the roasting tin and simmer to thicken. Season and stir in a knob of butter. Garnish the turkey with watercress. Pour the gravy into a serving jug and serve separately.

Cassoulet

If ever there was a dish that exemplifies farmhouse cooking,
it is this famous French casserole.

INGREDIENTS

675 g / 1½ lb / 3½ cups dried haricot
beans
900 g / 2 lb belly pork, preferably
salted
4 large duck breasts
60 ml / 4 tbsp olive oil
2 onions, chopped
6 garlic cloves, crushed
2 bay leaves
¼ tsp ground cloves
60 ml / 4 tbsp tomato purée
8 good-quality sausages
4 tomatoes, skinned and quartered
75 g / 3 oz / 1½ cups day-old white
breadcrumbs
salt and freshly ground black pepper

Serves 6–8

1

Put the beans in a large bowl and cover
with plenty of cold water. Leave to soak
overnight. If using salted belly pork, soak
it overnight in water, too.

2

Drain the beans and put them in a large
saucepan with fresh water to cover. Cover
and bring to the boil. Boil rapidly for
10 minutes. Drain and set the beans aside.

3

Drain the pork and cut it into large pieces,
discarding the rind. Halve the duck breasts.
Heat 30 ml / 2 tbsp of the oil in a frying
pan and fry the pork in batches, until
it is browned.

NOTE

You can easily alter the proportions and
types of meat and vegetables in a cassoulet.
Turnips, carrots and celeriac make suitable
vegetable substitutes while cubed lamb and
goose can replace the pork and duck.

4

Put the beans in a large, heavy-based
saucepan with the onions, garlic, bay leaves,
ground cloves and tomato purée. Stir in the
browned pork and just cover with water.
Bring to the boil, then reduce the heat to
the lowest setting and simmer, covered, for
about 1½ hours until the beans are tender.

5

Preheat the oven to 180°C / 350°F / Gas
Mark 4. Heat the rest of the oil in a frying
pan and fry the duck breasts and sausages
until browned. Cut the sausages into
smaller pieces. Transfer the bean mixture to
a large casserole. Stir in the fried sausages
and duck breasts and quartered tomatoes,
with salt and pepper to taste.

6

Sprinkle with an even layer of breadcrumbs.
Bake for 45 minutes to 1 hour until the
crust is golden. Serve hot.

Spicy Duck Breasts with Red Plums

Duck breasts can be bought separately, which makes this dish very easy to prepare.

INGREDIENTS

*4 duck breasts, 175 g / 6 oz
each, skinned
salt
2 tsp stick cinnamon, crushed
50 g / 2 oz butter
1 tbsp plum brandy (or Cognac)
250 ml / 8 fl oz chicken stock
250 ml / 8 fl oz double cream
pepper
6 fresh red plums, stoned and sliced
6 sprigs coriander leaves, plus some
extra to garnish*

Serves 4

1

Preheat the oven to 190°C/375°F/Gas Mark 5. Score the duck breasts and sprinkle with salt. Press the crushed cinnamon on to both sides of the duck breasts. Melt half the butter in a pan and fry them on both sides to seal, then place in an ovenproof dish with the butter and bake for 6–7 minutes.

2

Remove the dish from the oven and return the contents to the pan. Add the brandy and set it alight. When the flames have died down, remove from the pan and keep warm. Add the stock and cream to the pan and simmer gently until reduced and thick. Adjust the seasoning.

3

Reserve a few plum slices for garnishing. In a pan, melt the other half of the butter and fry the plums and coriander, just enough to cook the fruit through. Slice the duck breasts and pour some sauce around each one, then garnish with slices of plum and chopped coriander.

Duck Stew with Olives

*In this traditional method of preparing duck the sweetness of the shallots
balances the saltiness of the olives.*

INGREDIENTS

*2 ducks, about 1.4 kg / 3¼ lb each,
quartered, or 8 duck leg quarters
225 g / 8 oz / 1½ cups shallots, peeled
30 ml / 2 tbsp plain flour
350 ml / 12 fl oz / 1½ cups dry red wine
475 ml / 16 fl oz / 2 cups duck or
chicken stock
1 bouquet garni
115 g / 4 oz / 1 cup stoned green or
black olives, or a combination
salt, if needed, and freshly ground
black pepper*

Serves 6–8

1

Put the duck portions, skin side down, in a
large frying pan. Cook over a medium heat
for 10–12 minutes until well browned,
then turn to colour evenly. Cook in batches
if necessary.

2

Pour 15 ml / 1 tbsp of the duck fat into a
large, flameproof casserole. Place the
casserole over a medium heat and cook the
shallots until evenly browned, stirring
frequently. Sprinkle with the flour and cook
for 2 minutes more, stirring frequently.

3

Stir in the wine, then add the duck pieces,
stock and bouquet garni. Bring to the boil,
then reduce the heat, cover and simmer for
about 40 minutes, stirring occasionally.

4

Rinse the olives in several changes of cold
water. If they are very salty, put them in a
saucepan, cover with water and bring to the
boil, then drain and rinse. Add the stoned
olives to the casserole and continue
cooking for 20 minutes more, until the
duck is very tender.

5

Transfer the duck pieces, shallots and olives
to a plate. Strain the cooking liquid, skim
off all the fat and return the liquid to the
pan. Boil to reduce by about one-third,
then adjust the seasoning and return the
duck and vegetables to the casserole.
Simmer gently for a few minutes to heat
through and serve.

Duck and Chestnut Casserole

Serve this casserole with a mixture of mashed potatoes and celeriac,
to soak up the rich duck juices.

INGREDIENTS

1.75 kg / 4½ lb duck
45 ml / 3 tbsp olive oil
175 g / 6 oz small onions
50 g / 2 oz field mushrooms
50 g / 2 oz shiitake mushrooms
300 ml / ½ pint / 1¼ cups
red wine
300 ml / ½ pint / 1¼ cups
beef stock
225 g / 8 oz canned, peeled,
unsweetened chestnuts, drained
salt and freshly ground
black pepper

Serves 4–6

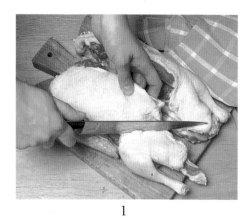

1

Joint the duck into eight pieces. Heat the oil
in a large frying pan and brown the duck
pieces. Remove from the frying pan.

2

Add the onions to the pan and brown them
well for 10 minutes.

3

Add the mushrooms and cook for a few
minutes more. Deglaze the pan with the
red wine and boil to reduce the volume
by half. Meanwhile, preheat the oven to
180°C / 350°F / Gas Mark 4.

4

Pour the wine and the stock into a
casserole. Replace the duck, add the
chestnuts, season well and cook in the oven
for 1½ hours.

Roast Wild Duck with Mushroom Sauce

*Wild duck is available in season from country markets and butchers specializing in game.
More strongly flavoured than the domestic bird, wild duck combines well with dried morels.*

INGREDIENTS

*2 x 1.2 kg / 2½ lb mallards, dressed
and barded weight
50 g / 2 oz / 4 tbsp butter
1 onion, halved and sliced
½ celery stick, chopped
1 small carrot, chopped
75 ml / 5 tbsp Madeira or sherry
10 large dried morel mushrooms
225 g / 8 oz wild mushrooms, trimmed
and sliced
600 ml / 1 pint / 2½ cups hot chicken
stock
1 fresh thyme sprig
10 ml / 2 tsp wine vinegar
salt and freshly ground black pepper
parsley sprigs and carrot matchsticks,
to garnish
game chips, to serve*

Serves 4

1

Preheat the oven to 190°C / 375°F / Gas
Mark 5. Season the ducks with salt and
pepper. Heat half the butter in a shallow
pan and fry the onion, celery and carrot for
5 minutes. Using a slotted spoon, transfer
the vegetables to a flameproof casserole
that is large enough to hold both ducks
side by side.

2

Add the remaining butter to the shallow
pan. When it is hot, brown the ducks.
Place them in the casserole. Pour the
Madeira or sherry into the pan and bring to
the boil. Pour this liquid over the birds.
Bake in the oven for 40 minutes.

3

Tie all the mushrooms in a piece of muslin.
Add the stock and thyme to the casserole.
Immerse the muslin bag in the liquid. Cover
and return to the oven for 40 minutes more.

4

Transfer the birds to a serving platter and
keep hot; set the mushrooms aside. Remove
the thyme from the braising liquid, then
purée the vegetables and liquid. Pour the
purée back into the casserole and stir the
mushrooms into the sauce. Add the vinegar
and seasoning and heat through gently.
Garnish the ducks with parsley and carrot.
Serve with game chips and mushroom sauce.

Guinea Fowl with Cabbage

Guinea fowl is a domesticated relative of pheasant, so pheasant or even chicken can be used in this recipe.

INGREDIENTS

15 ml / 1 tbsp vegetable oil
1.2–1.4 kg / 2½–3 lb guinea fowl, tied
15 g / ½ oz / 1 tbsp butter
1 large onion, halved and sliced
1 large carrot, halved and sliced
1 large leek, sliced
450 g / 1 lb green cabbage, such as Savoy, sliced or chopped
120 ml / 4 fl oz / ½ cup dry white wine
120 ml / 4 fl oz / ½ cup chicken stock
1 or 2 garlic cloves, finely chopped
salt and freshly ground black pepper

Serves 4

1

Preheat the oven to 180°C / 350°F / Gas Mark 4. Heat half the oil in a large, flameproof casserole and cook the guinea fowl until golden brown on all sides. Transfer to a plate.

2

Pour out the fat from the casserole and add the remaining oil with the butter. Cook the onion, carrot and leek over a low heat for 5 minutes, stirring occasionally. Add the cabbage and cook for about 3–4 minutes until slightly wilted, stirring occasionally. Season the vegetables with salt and pepper.

3

Place the guinea fowl on its side on the vegetables. Add the wine and bring to the boil, then add the stock and garlic. Cover and transfer to the oven. Cook for 25 minutes, then turn the bird on to the other side and cook for 20–25 minutes more, until it is tender and the juices run clear when the thickest part of the thigh is pierced with a knife.

4

Transfer the bird to a board and leave to stand for 5–10 minutes, then cut into four or eight pieces. With a slotted spoon, transfer the cabbage to a warmed serving dish and place the guinea fowl on top. Skim any fat from the cooking juices and serve separately.

Roast Pheasant with Port

Many farmers – and their fortunate friends – have a regular supply of pheasant in the shooting season. This is an excellent way of cooking them.

*2 oven-ready hen pheasants, about
675 g / 1½ lb each
50 g / 2 oz / 4 tbsp butter, softened
8 fresh thyme sprigs
2 bay leaves
6 rindless streaky bacon rashers
15 ml / 1 tbsp plain flour
175 ml / 6 fl oz / ¾ cup game or
chicken stock, plus more if needed
15 ml / 1 tbsp redcurrant jelly
45–60 ml / 3–4 tbsp port
freshly ground black pepper*

Serves 4

1

Preheat the oven to 230°C / 450°F / Gas Mark 8. Line a large roasting tin with a sheet of strong foil large enough to enclose the pheasants. Lightly brush the foil with oil.

2

Wipe the pheasants with damp kitchen paper and remove any extra fat or skin. Using your fingertips, carefully loosen the skin of the breasts. Spread the butter between the skin and breast meat of each bird. Tie the legs securely with string, then lay the thyme sprigs and a bay leaf over the breast of each bird.

3

Lay the bacon over the breasts, place the birds in the foil-lined tin and season with pepper. Bring up the foil and enclose the birds. Roast for 20 minutes, then reduce the oven temperature to 190°C / 375°F / Gas Mark 5 and cook for 40 minutes more.

4

Uncover the birds and roast 10–15 minutes more. Transfer the birds to a board and leave to stand for 10 minutes before carving.

5

Pour the juices into the roasting tin and skim off any fat. Sprinkle in the flour and stir over a medium heat until smooth. Whisk in the stock and redcurrant jelly and bring to the boil. Simmer until the sauce thickens slightly, then stir in the port and adjust the seasoning. Strain and serve with the pheasants.

Braised Pheasant with Ceps, Chestnuts and Bacon

Towards the end of their season pheasant can be a little tough, so are best braised. Try this delicious casserole enriched with wild mushrooms and chestnuts.

INGREDIENTS

2 mature pheasants
50 g / 2 oz / 4 tbsp butter
75 ml / 5 tbsp brandy
12 button or pickling onions, peeled
1 celery stick, chopped
50 g / 2 oz rindless unsmoked streaky bacon, cut into strips
20 g / ¾ oz / 3 tbsp plain flour
500 ml / 18 fl oz / 2¼ cups hot chicken stock
175 g / 6 oz / 1½ cups peeled chestnuts
350 g / 12 oz / 3 cups fresh ceps or other wild mushrooms, trimmed and sliced, or 15 g / ½ oz / ¼ cup dried ceps, soaked in warm water for 20 minutes
15 ml / 1 tbsp lemon juice
salt and freshly ground black pepper
watercress sprigs, to garnish

Serves 4

2

Melt the remaining butter. Lightly brown the onions, celery and bacon. Stir in the flour, cook for 1 minute, then gradually stir in the stock. Add the chestnuts and mushrooms, then replace the pheasants and their juices. Bring to a gentle simmer, cover and cook in the oven for 1½ hours.

3

Transfer the pheasants and vegetables to a serving plate. Skim off any fat from the sauce, bring it back to the boil, add the lemon juice and season to taste. Pour the sauce into a jug and garnish the birds with watercress sprigs.

1

Preheat the oven to 170°C / 325°F / Gas Mark 3. Season the pheasants with salt and pepper. Melt half the butter in a large, flameproof casserole and brown the birds all over. Transfer to a shallow dish. Pour off the cooking fat and return the casserole to the heat. Stir the sediment until it has browned. Stand back and add the brandy (the sudden flames will die down quickly). Stir to incorporate the sediment, then pour the juices over the pheasant.

Pigeon Pie

This recipe is based upon a traditional dish, a filo pie filled with an unusual but delicious mixture of pigeon, eggs, spices and nuts. Chicken can be used instead of pigeon.

INGREDIENTS

3 pigeons
50 g / 2 oz / 4 tbsp butter
1 onion, chopped
1 cinnamon stick
½ tsp ground ginger
30 ml / 2 tbsp chopped fresh coriander
45 ml / 3 tbsp chopped fresh parsley
pinch of ground turmeric
15 ml / 1 tbsp caster sugar
¼ tsp ground cinnamon
115 g / 4 oz / 1 cup toasted almonds, finely chopped
6 eggs, beaten
salt and freshly ground black pepper
cinnamon and icing sugar, to garnish

For the pastry
175 g / 6 oz / ¾ cup butter, melted
16 sheets filo pastry
1 egg yolk

Serves 6

1

Wash the pigeons and place them in a heavy-based pan with the butter, onion, cinnamon stick, ginger, coriander, parsley and turmeric. Season with salt and pepper. Add just enough water to cover and bring to the boil. Reduce the heat, cover and simmer gently for about 1 hour, until the pigeon flesh is very tender.

2

Strain off the stock and reserve. Skin and bone the pigeons, and shred the flesh into bite-size pieces. Preheat the oven to 180°C / 350°F / Gas Mark 4. Mix the sugar, cinnamon and almonds in a bowl.

3

Measure 150 ml / ¼ pint / ⅔ cup of the reserved stock into a small pan. Add the eggs and mix well. Stir over a low heat until creamy and very thick and almost set. Season with salt and pepper.

4

Brush a 30 cm / 12 in diameter ovenproof dish with some of the melted butter and lay the first sheet of pastry in the dish. Brush this with butter and continue with five more sheets of pastry. Cover with the almond mixture, then half the egg mixture. Moisten with a little stock.

5

Layer four more sheets of filo pastry, brushing with butter as before. Lay the pigeon meat on top, then add the remaining egg mixture and more stock. Cover with all the remaining pastry, brushing each sheet with butter, and tuck in any overlap.

6

Brush the pie with egg yolk and bake for 40 minutes. Raise the oven temperature to 200°C / 400°F / Gas Mark 6, and bake for 15 minutes more, until the pastry is crisp and golden. Garnish with cinnamon and icing sugar in a lattice design. Serve hot.

Rabbit Sauté

Rabbit has always been a farmhouse favourite. Townies eager to try this recipe should look out for packs of rabbit portions, sold at the supermarket.

INGREDIENTS

675 g / 1½ lb rabbit portions
300 ml / ½ pint / 1¼ cups dry white wine
15 ml / 1 tbsp sherry vinegar
several fresh oregano sprigs
2 bay leaves
1 fresh red chilli
90 ml / 6 tbsp olive oil
175 g / 6 oz baby onions or shallots, peeled
4 garlic cloves, sliced
10 ml / 2 tsp paprika
150 ml / ¼ pint / ⅔ cup chicken stock
salt and freshly ground black pepper
flat leaf parsley sprigs, to garnish

Serves 4

1

Put the rabbit in a bowl. Add the wine, vinegar, oregano and bay leaves and toss lightly. Cover and marinate for several hours or overnight.

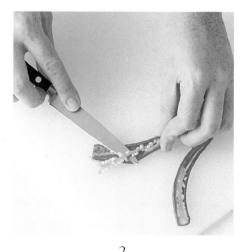

2

Remove the seeds from the chilli and chop it finely. Set it aside. Drain the rabbit portions, reserving the marinade, and pat dry on kitchen paper. Heat the oil in a large frying pan and fry the rabbit on all sides until golden, then remove with a slotted spoon. Fry the onions until beginning to colour.

NOTE
If more convenient, bake the stew in an ovenproof dish at 180°C / 350°F / Gas Mark 4 for about 50 minutes.

3

Remove the onions from the pan and add the chilli, garlic and paprika. Cook, stirring, for about 1 minute. Add the reserved marinade, with the stock. Season lightly.

4

Return the rabbit to the pan with the onions. Bring to the boil, then reduce the heat, cover and simmer for about 45 minutes until the rabbit is tender. Serve, garnished with a few sprigs of flat leaf parsley, if you like.

Casseroled Rabbit with Thyme

This is the sort of home cooking found in farmhouse kitchens and cosy neighbourhood restaurants in France, where rabbit is treated much like chicken and enjoyed frequently.

INGREDIENTS

40 g / 1½ oz / 6 tbsp plain flour
1.2 kg / 2½ lb rabbit, cut into 8 portions
15 g / ½ oz / 1 tbsp butter
15 ml / 1 tbsp olive oil
250 ml / 8 fl oz / 1 cup red wine
350–475 ml / 12–16 fl oz / 1½–2 cups chicken stock
15 ml / 1 tbsp fresh thyme leaves
1 bay leaf
2 garlic cloves, finely chopped
10–15 ml / 2–3 tsp Dijon mustard
salt and freshly ground black pepper

Serves 4

1

Put the flour in a polythene bag and season with salt and pepper. One at a time, drop the rabbit pieces into the bag and shake to coat them with flour. Tap off the excess, then discard any remaining flour.

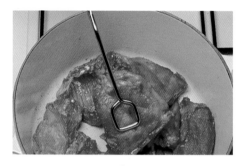

2

Melt the butter and oil in a flameproof casserole. Cook the rabbit pieces until golden.

3

Pour in the wine and boil for 1 minute, then add enough of the stock just to cover the meat. Add the herbs and garlic. Cover and simmer gently for 1 hour.

4

Stir in the mustard. Lift the rabbit pieces on to a serving platter. Season the sauce, then strain it over the rabbit.

Farmhouse Venison Pie

This satisfying pie combines venison in a rich gravy with a potato and parsnip topping.

INGREDIENTS

45 ml / 3 tbsp sunflower oil
1 onion, chopped
1 garlic clove, crushed
3 rindless streaky bacon rashers,
chopped
675 g / 1½ lb minced venison
115 g / 4 oz / 1 cup button
mushrooms, chopped
30 ml / 2 tbsp plain flour
475 ml / 16 fl oz / 2 cups beef stock
150 ml / ¼ pint / ⅔ cup ruby port
2 bay leaves
5 ml / 1 tsp chopped fresh thyme
5 ml / 1 tsp Dijon mustard
15 ml / 1 tbsp redcurrant jelly
675 g / 1½ lb potatoes, peeled and cut
into large chunks
450 g / 1 lb parsnips, peeled and cut
into large chunks
1 egg yolk
50 g / 2 oz / 4 tbsp butter
grated nutmeg
45 ml / 3 tbsp chopped fresh parsley
salt and freshly ground black pepper

Serves 4

2

Meanwhile, preheat the oven to 200°C / 400°F / Gas Mark 6. Bring a saucepan of lightly salted water to the boil and cook the potatoes and parsnips for 20 minutes or until tender. Drain and mash, then beat in the egg yolk, butter, nutmeg and chopped parsley. Season to taste with salt and pepper.

3

Spoon the venison mixture into a large pie dish. Level the surface. Spread the potato and parsnip mixture over the meat and bake for 30–40 minutes, until piping hot and golden brown. Serve at once.

1

Heat the oil in a large frying pan and fry the onion, garlic and bacon for about 5 minutes. Add the venison and mushrooms and cook for a few minutes, stirring, until browned. Stir in the flour and cook for 1–2 minutes, then add the stock, port, herbs, mustard, redcurrant jelly and seasoning. Bring to the boil, cover and simmer for 30–40 minutes, until tender.

Meat Dishes

In farmhouses all over the world, main meals mean meat. Robust roasts, meat loaves, plaits and pies are very popular, but it is the stew that reigns supreme. Simmered for hours in rich stock flavoured with wine, herbs and aromatic vegetables, meat becomes meltingly tender. The following section is packed with hearty meat recipes to choose from to suit the time available and the occasion in mind.

Lamb Stew with Vegetables

This farmhouse stew is made with lamb and a selection of young tender spring vegetables such as carrots, new potatoes, baby onions, peas, French beans and especially turnips!

INGREDIENTS

*60 ml / 4 tbsp vegetable oil
1.5 kg / 3–3½ lb lamb shoulder, trimmed and cut into 5 cm / 2 in pieces
120 ml / 4 fl oz / ½ cup water
45–60 ml / 3–4 tbsp plain flour
1 litre / 1¾ pints / 4 cups lamb stock
1 large bouquet garni
3 garlic cloves, lightly crushed
3 ripe tomatoes, skinned, seeded and chopped
5 ml / 1 tsp tomato purée
675 g / 1½ lb small potatoes, peeled or scrubbed
12 baby carrots, scrubbed*

*115 g / 4 oz French beans, cut into 5 cm / 2 in pieces
25 g / 1 oz / 2 tbsp butter
12–18 baby onions or shallots, peeled
6 medium turnips, quartered
30 ml / 2 tbsp granulated sugar
¼ tsp dried thyme
175 g / 6 oz / 1¼ cups peas
50 g / 2 oz / ½ cup mangetouts
salt and freshly ground pepper
45 ml / 3 tbsp chopped fresh parsley or coriander, to garnish*

Serves 6

1

Heat half the oil in a large, heavy-based frying pan. Brown the lamb in batches, adding more oil if needed, and place it in a large, flameproof casserole. Add 45 ml / 3 tbsp of the water to the pan and boil for about 1 minute, stirring and scraping the base of the pan, then pour the liquid into the casserole.

2

Sprinkle the flour over the browned meat in the casserole and set it over a medium heat. Cook for 3–5 minutes until browned. Stir in the stock, the bouquet garni, garlic, tomatoes and tomato purée. Season with salt and pepper.

3

Bring to the boil over a high heat. Skim the surface, reduce the heat and simmer, stirring occasionally, for about 1 hour until the meat is tender. Cool the stew to room temperature, cover and chill overnight.

4

About 1½ hours before serving, take the casserole from the fridge, lift off the solid fat and blot the surface with kitchen paper to remove all traces of fat. Set the casserole over a medium heat and bring to a simmer. Cook the potatoes in a pan of boiling, salted water for 15–20 minutes, then transfer to a bowl and add the carrots to the same water. Cook for 4–5 minutes and transfer to the same bowl. Add the French beans and boil for 2–3 minutes. Transfer to the bowl with the other vegetables.

5

(Left) Melt the butter in a heavy-based frying pan and add the onions and turnips with a further 45 ml / 3 tbsp water. Cover and cook for 4–5 minutes. Stir in the sugar and thyme and cook until the vegetables are caramelized. Transfer them to the bowl of vegetables. Add the remaining water to the pan. Boil for 1 minute, incorporating the sediment, then add to the lamb.

6

When the lamb and gravy are hot, add the cooked vegetables to the stew and stir gently to distribute. Stir in the peas and mangetouts and cook for 5 minutes until they turn a bright green, then stir in 30 ml / 2 tbsp of the parsley or coriander. Pour the stew into a large, warmed serving dish. Scatter over the remaining parsley or coriander and serve.

Roast Leg of Lamb with Wild Mushroom Stuffing

*Removing the thigh bone creates a cavity that can be filled with
a wild mushroom stuffing – the perfect treat for Sunday lunch.*

INGREDIENTS

*1.75 kg / 4–4½ lb leg of lamb, boned
salt and freshly ground black pepper
watercress, to garnish*

For the wild mushroom stuffing
*25 g / 1 oz / 2 tbsp butter
1 shallot or small onion, chopped
225 g / 8 oz / 2 cups assorted wild
and cultivated mushrooms*

*½ garlic clove, crushed
1 fresh thyme sprig, chopped
25 g / 1 oz crustless white
bread, diced
2 egg yolks*

For the wild mushroom gravy
*60 ml / 4 tbsp red wine
400 ml / 14 fl oz / 1⅔ cups hot*

*chicken stock
5 g / 2 tbsp dried ceps, soaked in
boiling water for 20 minutes
20 ml / 4 tsp cornflour
5 ml / 1 tsp Dijon mustard
15 ml / 1 tbsp water
½ tsp wine vinegar
knob of butter*

Serves 4

1

Preheat the oven to 200°C / 400°F / Gas
Mark 6. To make the stuffing, melt the
butter in a large, non-stick frying pan and
gently fry the shallot or onion without
colouring. Add the mushrooms, garlic and
thyme. Stir until the mushroom juices
begin to run, then increase the heat so that
they evaporate completely.

4

Place the lamb in a roasting tin. Roast for
15 minutes per 450 g / 1 lb for rare meat
and 20 minutes per 450 g / 1 lb for
medium-rare. A 1.8 kg / 4 lb leg will take
1 hour 20 minutes if cooked medium-rare.

2

Transfer the mushrooms to a mixing bowl
and add the bread and egg yolks. Season
with salt and pepper and mix well. Allow
to cool slightly.

5

Transfer the lamb to a warmed serving
plate. Spoon off all excess fat from the
roasting tin and brown the sediment over a
medium heat. Add the wine and stir in the
chicken stock and the mushrooms, with
their soaking liquid.

3

Season the inside of the lamb cavity, then
spoon in the stuffing. Tie up the end with
fine string and then tie around the joint so
that it does not lose its shape.

6

Mix the cornflour and mustard in a cup;
blend in the water. Stir into the stock and
thicken. Add the vinegar. Season and stir in
the butter. Garnish the lamb with
watercress and serve with the wild
mushroom gravy.

Lamb with Mint and Lemon

Lamb has been served with mint for many years – it is a great combination.

INGREDIENTS

8 lamb steaks, 225 g / 8 oz each
grated rind and juice of 1 lemon
2 cloves garlic, peeled and crushed
2 spring onions, finely chopped
2 tsp finely chopped fresh mint
leaves, plus some leaves for
garnishing
4 tbsp extra virgin olive oil
salt and black pepper

Serves 8

1

Make a marinade for the lamb by mixing all the other ingredients and seasoning to taste. Place the lamb steaks in a shallow dish and cover with the marinade. Refrigerate overnight.

2

Grill the lamb under a high heat until just cooked, basting with the marinade occasionally during cooking. Turn once during cooking. Serve garnished with fresh mint leaves.

Lamb Pie with Pear, Ginger and Mint Sauce

Cooking lamb with fruit is an idea taken from traditional Persian cuisine.

INGREDIENTS

*1 boned mid-loin of lamb, 1 kg / 2 lb
after boning
salt and pepper
8 large sheets filo pastry
25 g / 1 oz / scant 2 tbsp butter*

*For the stuffing
1 tbsp butter
1 small onion, chopped
115 g / 4 oz wholemeal breadcrumbs
grated rind of 1 lemon
170 g / 6 oz drained canned pears from*

*a 400 g / 14 oz can (rest
of can, and juice, used for sauce)
¼ tsp ground ginger
1 small egg, beaten
skewers, string and large needle to
make roll*

*For the sauce
rest of can of pears, including juice
2 tsp finely chopped fresh mint*

Serves 6

1

Prepare the stuffing. Melt the butter in a pan and add the onion, cooking until soft. Preheat the oven to 180°C / 350°F / Gas Mark 4. Put the butter and onion into a mixing bowl and add the breadcrumbs, lemon rind, pears and ginger. Season lightly and add enough beaten egg to bind.

2

Spread the loin out flat, fat side down, and season. Place the stuffing along the middle of the loin and roll carefully, holding with skewers while you sew it together with string. Heat a large baking pan in the oven and brown the loin slowly on all sides. This will take 20–30 minutes. Leave to cool, and store in the refrigerator until needed.

3

Preheat the oven to 200°C / 400°F / Gas Mark 6. Take two sheets of filo pastry and brush with melted butter. Overlap by about 13 cm / 5 in to make a square. Place the next two sheets on top and brush with butter. Continue until all the pastry has been used.

4

Place the roll of lamb diagonally across one corner of the pastry, without overlapping the sides. Fold the corner over the lamb, fold in the sides, and brush the pastry well with melted butter. Roll to the far corner of the sheet. Place join side down on a buttered baking sheet and brush all over with the rest of the melted butter. Bake for about 30 minutes or until golden brown.

5

Blend the remaining pears with their juice and the mint, and serve with the lamb.

Lamb and Leeks with Mint and Spring Onions

If you do not have any home-made chicken stock, use a good quality ready-made stock rather than a stock cube.

INGREDIENTS

*2 tbsp sunflower oil
2 kg / 4 lb lamb (fillet or boned leg)
10 spring onions, thickly sliced
3 leeks, thickly sliced
1 tbsp flour
150 ml / ¼ pint white wine
300 ml / ½ pint chicken stock
1 tbsp tomato purée
1 tbsp sugar
salt and pepper
2 tbsp fresh mint leaves, finely
chopped, plus a few more to garnish
115 g / 4 oz dried pears
1 kg / 2 lb potatoes, peeled and sliced
30 g / 1¼ oz melted butter*

Serves 6

1

Heat the oil and fry the cubed lamb to seal it. Transfer to a casserole. Preheat the oven to 180°C/350°F/Gas Mark 4.

2

Fry the onions and leeks for 1 minute, stir in the flour and cook for another minute. Add the wine and stock and bring to the boil. Add the tomato purée, sugar, salt and pepper with the mint and chopped pears and pour into the casserole. Stir the mixture. Arrange the sliced potatoes on top and brush with the melted butter.

3

Cover and bake for 1½ hours. Then increase the temperature to 200°C/400°F/Gas Mark 6, cook for a further 30 minutes, uncovered, to brown the potatoes. Garnish with mint leaves.

Pork Sausage and Puff Pastry Plait

Country butchers sell a wonderful variety of sausages, including venison, pork and apple, and herb. All taste delicious when wrapped around a wild mushroom filling and baked in pastry.

· 50 g / 2 oz / 4 tbsp butter
½ garlic clove, crushed
15 ml / 1 tbsp chopped fresh thyme
450 g / 1 lb assorted wild and
cultivated mushrooms, sliced
50 g / 2 oz / 1 cup fresh white
breadcrumbs
75 ml / 5 tbsp chopped fresh parsley
350 g / 12 oz puff pastry
675 g / 1½ lb best pork sausages
1 egg, beaten with a pinch of salt
salt and freshly ground black pepper

Serves 4

3

Make a series of slanting 2.5 cm / 1 in cuts in the pastry on either side of the filling. Fold each end of the pastry over the filling, moisten the pastry with beaten egg and then cross the top with alternate strips of pastry from each side. Allow the plait to rest for 40 minutes. Preheat the oven to 180°C / 350°F / Gas Mark 4. Brush the plait with a little more egg and bake for 1 hour.

1

Melt the butter in a large frying pan and soften the garlic, thyme and mushrooms gently for 5–6 minutes. When the mushroom juices begin to run, increase the heat to drive off the liquid, then stir in the breadcrumbs, parsley and seasoning.

2

Roll out the pastry on a floured surface to a 36 x 25 cm / 14 x 10 in rectangle. Place on a large baking sheet. Skin the sausages. Place half of the sausagemeat in a 13 cm / 5 in strip along the centre of the pastry. Cover with the mushroom mixture, then with the rest of the sausagemeat.

Pork and Black Bean Stew

This simple Spanish stew uses a few robust ingredients to create a deliciously intense flavour.

INGREDIENTS

*275 g / 10 oz / 1½ cups black beans,
soaked overnight
675 g / 1½ lb boneless belly pork
rashers
60 ml / 4 tbsp olive oil
350 g / 12 oz baby onions or shallots
2 celery sticks, thickly sliced
10 ml / 2 tsp paprika
150 g / 5 oz chorizo sausage, chopped
600 ml / 1 pint / 2½ cups light
chicken or vegetable stock
2 green peppers, seeded and cut into
large pieces
salt and freshly ground pepper*

Serves 5–6

1

Preheat the oven to 160°C / 325°F / Gas Mark 3. Drain the beans, place them in a saucepan and cover with fresh water. Bring to the boil, boil rapidly for 10 minutes, then drain. Cut away any rind from the pork and cut the meat into large chunks.

2

Heat the oil in a large frying pan and fry the onions or shallots and celery for 3 minutes. Add the pork and fry for 5–10 minutes until the pork is browned. Stir in the paprika and chorizo and fry for 2 minutes more. Transfer to an ovenproof dish, add the beans and mix well.

3

Add the stock to the pan and bring to the boil. Season lightly, then pour over the meat and beans. Cover and bake for 1 hour, then stir in the green peppers. Bake for 15 minutes more and serve hot.

NOTE

This is a good-natured stew which works well with any winter vegetable. Try adding chunks of leek, turnip, celeriac and even little potatoes.

Pork and Sausage Casserole

*This dish is based on a rural Spanish recipe. You should be able to find the butifarra
sausages in a delicatessen but, if not, sweet Italian sausages will do.*

INGREDIENTS

*30 ml / 2 tbsp olive oil
4 boneless pork chops, about 175 g / 6 oz
4 butifarra or sweet Italian sausages
1 onion, chopped
2 garlic cloves, chopped
120 ml / 4 fl oz / ½ cup dry white wine
4 plum tomatoes, chopped
1 bay leaf
30 ml / 2 tbsp chopped fresh parsley
salt and freshly ground black pepper
green salad and baked potatoes, to serve*

Serves 4

NOTE
Vine tomatoes, which are making a
welcome appearance in our supermarkets,
can be used instead of plum tomatoes.

1

Heat the oil in a large, deep frying pan.
Cook the pork chops over a high heat until
browned on both sides, then transfer
to a plate.

2

Add the sausages, onion and garlic to the
pan and cook over a moderate heat until
the sausages are browned and the onion
softened, turning the sausages two or three
times during cooking. Return the chops
to the pan.

3

Stir in the wine, tomatoes and bay leaf, and
season with salt and pepper. Add the
parsley. Cover the pan and cook for
30 minutes.

4

Remove the sausages from the pan and cut
into thick slices. Return them to the pan
and heat through. Serve hot, accompanied
by a green salad and baked potatoes.

Country Pie

A classic raised pie. It takes quite a long time to make,
but is a perfect winter treat.

INGREDIENTS

1 small duck
1 small chicken
350 g / 12 oz pork belly, minced
1 egg, lightly beaten
2 shallots, finely chopped
½ tsp ground cinnamon
½ tsp grated nutmeg
5 ml / 1 tsp Worcestershire sauce
finely grated rind of 1 lemon
½ tsp freshly ground black pepper
150 ml / ¼ pint / ⅔ cup red wine
175 g / 6 oz ham, cut into cubes
salt and freshly ground
black pepper

For the jelly
all the meat bones and trimmings
2 carrots
1 onion
2 celery sticks
15 ml / 1 tbsp red wine
1 bay leaf
1 whole clove
1 sachet of gelatine
(about 15 g / 1 oz)

For the pastry
225 g / 8 oz / 1 cup hard white fat
300 ml / ½ pint / 1¼ cups boiling
water
675 g / 1½ lb / 6 cups plain flour
1 egg, lightly beaten with a
pinch of salt

Serves 12

1

Cut as much meat from the raw duck and
chicken as possible, removing the skin and
sinews. Cut the duck and chicken breasts
into cubes and set them aside.

2

Mix the rest of the duck and chicken meat
with the minced pork, egg, shallots, spices,
Worcestershire sauce, lemon rind and salt
and pepper. Add the red wine and leave for
about 15 minutes for the flavours to develop.

3

To make the jelly, place the meat bones and
trimmings, carrots, onion, celery, wine, bay
leaf and clove in a large pan and cover with
2.75 litres / 5 pints / 12½ cups of water.
Bring to the boil, skimming off any scum,
and simmer gently for 2½ hours.

4

To make the pastry, place the fat and water
in a pan and bring to the boil. Sieve the flour
and a pinch of salt into a bowl and pour on the
liquid. Mix with a wooden spoon, and,
when the dough is cool enough to handle,
knead it well and let it sit in a warm place,
covered with a cloth, for 20–30 minutes or
until you are ready to use it. Preheat the
oven to 200°C / 400°F / Gas Mark 6.

5

Grease a 25 cm / 10 in loose-based deep cake tin. Roll out about two-thirds of the pastry thinly enough to line the cake tin. Make sure there are no holes and allow enough pastry to leave a little hanging over the top. Fill the pie with a layer of half the minced-pork mixture; then top this with a layer of the cubed duck and chicken breast-meat and cubes of ham. Top with the remaining minced pork. Brush the overhanging edges of pastry with water and cover with the remaining rolled-out pastry. Seal the edges well. Make two large holes in the top and decorate with any pastry trimmings.

6

Bake the pie for 30 minutes. Brush the top with the egg and salt mixture. Turn down the oven to 180°C / 350°F / Gas Mark 4. After 30 minutes loosely cover the pie with foil to prevent the top getting too brown, and bake it for a further 1 hour.

7

Strain the stock after 2½ hours. Let it cool and remove the solidified layer of fat from the surface. Measure 600 ml / 1 pint / 2½ cups of stock. Heat it gently to just below boiling point and whisk the gelatine into it until no lumps are left. Add the remaining strained stock and leave to cool.

8

When the pie is cool, place a funnel through one of the holes and pour in as much of the stock as possible, letting it come up to the holes in the crust. Leave to set for at least 24 hours before slicing and serving.

Slow-cooked Beef Stew

In its native Provence, this is called a daube, and takes the name from the daubière, the earthenware pot it was traditionally cooked in. It is improved by being cooked a day ahead.

INGREDIENTS

30–60 ml / 2–4 tbsp olive oil
225 g / 8 oz lean salt pork or thick-cut rindless streaky bacon, diced
1.75 kg / 4–4½ lb stewing beef, cut into 7.5 cm / 3 in pieces
750 ml / 1¼ pints / 3 cups red wine
4 carrots, thickly sliced
2 large onions, coarsely chopped
3 tomatoes, skinned, seeded and chopped
15 ml / 1 tbsp tomato purée
2–4 garlic cloves, very finely chopped
1 bouquet garni
5 ml / 1 tsp black peppercorns
1 small onion, studded with 4 cloves
grated rind and juice of 1 orange
30–45 ml / 2–3 tbsp chopped parsley
salt and freshly ground black pepper

Serves 6–8

1

Heat 30 ml / 2 tbsp of the olive oil in a large, heavy-based frying pan and cook the salt pork or bacon, stirring frequently, until the fat runs. Raise the heat and cook for 4–5 minutes more, until browned. Transfer with a slotted spoon to a large, flameproof casserole.

2

Add enough beef to the pan to fit easily in one layer. Cook for 6–8 minutes until browned, turning to colour all sides, then transfer the meat to the casserole. Brown the rest of the meat in the same way, adding a little more oil if needed.

3

Pour in the wine and, if needed, add water to cover the beef and bacon. Bring to the boil over a medium heat, skimming off any foam that rises to the surface.

4

Stir in the carrots, onions, tomatoes, tomato purée, garlic, bouquet garni, peppercorns and clove-studded onion. Cover tightly and simmer over a low heat for about 3 hours. Skim off any fat. Season, discard the bouquet garni and onion and stir in the orange rind and juice and the parsley.

Beef Casserole with Beans

This hearty casserole is slow cooked to ensure that the meat is beautifully tender.

INGREDIENTS

*225 g / 8 oz / 1¼ cups haricot or
butter beans, soaked overnight in water
30–60 ml / 2–4 tbsp oil
10 small onions, halved
2 carrots, diced
1.5 kg / 3–3½ lb stewing steak, cubed
6 small hard-boiled eggs in their shells
5 ml / 1 tsp paprika
5 ml / 1 tsp tomato purée
600 ml / 1 pint / 2½ cups boiling
water or beef stock
salt and freshly ground black pepper*

Serves 6–8

NOTE

If you have one, use a large slow cooker for
cooking the stew. You should not need to
add extra liquid.

3

Stir the paprika and tomato purée into the
oil left in the pan. Add a generous
sprinkling of salt and pepper and cook for
1 minute. Stir in the boiling water or stock
to incorporate the sediment, then pour the
mixture over the meat and eggs.

4

Cover the casserole and cook the cholent for
at least 8 hours or until the meat is very
tender, adding more liquid as needed. Take
out the eggs, remove the shells and return
them to the casserole before serving.

1

Preheat the oven to 110°C / 225°F / Gas
Mark ¼. Drain the beans, place them in a
saucepan and cover with fresh water. Bring
to the boil. Cook rapidly for 10 minutes,
skimming off the white froth and any bean
skins that come to the surface. Drain.

2

Heat half the oil in a frying pan and sauté the
onions for about 10 minutes, then transfer to
a casserole, with the carrots and beans. Heat
the remaining oil and brown the beef in
batches. Place it on top of the vegetables.
Tuck the eggs between the pieces of meat.

Beef Rib with Onion Sauce

Beef with a peppercorn crust, seared in a pan and then briefly roasted in the oven, feeds two hungry farm workers or four people with less hearty appetites. The onion sauce is superb.

INGREDIENTS

*1 beef rib with bone, about 1 kg /
2¼ lb and about 4 cm / 1½ in thick,
well trimmed of fat
5 ml / 1 tsp lightly crushed black
peppercorns
15 ml / 1 tbsp coarse sea salt, crushed
50 g / 2 oz / 4 tbsp butter
1 large red onion, sliced
120 ml / 4 fl oz / ½ cup fruity red
wine
120 ml / 4 fl oz / ½ cup beef stock
15–30 ml / 1–2 tbsp redcurrant jelly
¼ tsp dried thyme
30–45 ml / 2–3 tbsp olive oil
salt and freshly ground black pepper*

Serves 2–4

1

Wipe the beef with damp kitchen paper. Mix the crushed peppercorns with the crushed salt and press the mixture on to both sides of the meat, coating it completely. Leave to stand, loosely covered, for 30 minutes.

2

Meanwhile, make the sauce. Melt 40 g / 1½ oz / 3 tbsp of the butter in a saucepan and cook the onion for 3–5 minutes until softened. Add the wine, stock, redcurrant jelly and thyme and bring to the boil. Reduce the heat and simmer for 30–35 minutes until the liquid has evaporated and the sauce has thickened. Season with salt and pepper and keep hot.

3

Preheat the oven to 220°C / 425°F / Gas Mark 7. Melt the remaining butter with the oil in a heavy, ovenproof frying pan. Add the meat and sear over a high heat for 1–2 minutes on each side. Immediately place the pan in the oven and roast for 8–10 minutes. Transfer the beef to a board, cover loosely and leave to stand for 10 minutes. With a knife, loosen the meat from the rib bone, then carve into thick slices. Serve with the onion sauce.

Roast Beef with Mushrooms and Roasted Sweet Peppers

A substantial and warming dish for cold, dark evenings.

1.5 kg / 3–3½ lb piece of sirloin
15 ml / 1 tbsp olive oil
450 g / 1 lb small red peppers
115 g / 4 oz mushrooms
175 g / 6 oz thick-sliced pancetta
or smoked bacon, cubed
50 g / 2 oz / 2 tbsp plain flour
150 ml / ¼ pint / ⅔ cup full-
bodied red wine
300 ml / ½ pint / 1¼ cups beef stock
30 ml / 2 tbsp Marsala
10 ml / 2 tsp dried mixed herbs
salt and freshly ground
black pepper

Serves 8

1

Preheat the oven to 190°C/375°F/
Gas Mark 5. Season the meat well. Heat the
olive oil in a large frying pan. When very
hot, brown the meat on all sides. Place in a
large roasting tin and cook for 1¼ hours.

2

Put the red peppers in the oven to roast for
20 minutes, if small ones are available, or
45 minutes if large ones are used.

3

Near the end of the meat's cooking time,
prepare the gravy. Roughly chop the
mushroom caps and stems.

4

Heat the frying pan again and add the
pancetta or bacon. Cook until the fat runs
freely from the meat. Add the flour and cook
for a few minutes until browned.

5

Gradually stir in the red wine and the stock.
Bring to the boil, stirring. Lower the heat
and add the Marsala, herbs and seasoning.

6

Add the mushrooms to the pan and heat
through. Remove the sirloin from the oven
and leave to stand for 10 minutes before
carving it. Serve with the roasted peppers
and the hot gravy.

Traditional Beef Stew and Dumplings

This dish can cook in the oven while you go for a wintery walk to work up an appetite.

INGREDIENTS

25 g / 1 oz / 1 tbsp plain flour
1.2 kg / 2½ lb stewing steak,
cubed
30 ml / 2 tbsp olive oil
2 large onions, sliced
450 g / 1 lb carrots, sliced
300 ml / ½ pint / 1¼ cups
Guinness or dark beer
3 bay leaves
10 ml / 2 tsp brown sugar
3 fresh thyme sprigs
5 ml / 1 tsp cider vinegar
salt and freshly ground
black pepper

For the dumplings
115 g / 4 oz / ½ cup grated hard
white fat
225 g / 8 oz / 2 cups self-raising
flour
30 ml / 2 tbsp chopped mixed
fresh herbs
about 150 ml / ¼ pint / ⅔ cup
water

Serves 6

1

Preheat the oven to 160°C / 325°F /
Gas Mark 3. Season the flour and sprinkle
over the meat, tossing to coat.

2

Heat the oil in a large casserole and lightly
sauté the onions and carrots. Remove the
vegetables with a slotted spoon and
reserve them.

3

Brown the meat well in batches
in the casserole.

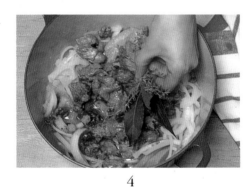

4

Return all the vegetables to the casserole and
add any leftover seasoned flour. Add the
Guinness or beer, bay leaves, sugar and
thyme. Bring the liquid to the boil and then
transfer to the oven. Leave the meat to cook
for 1 hour and 40 minutes, before making
the dumplings.

5

Mix the grated fat, flour and herbs together.
Add enough water to make a soft
sticky dough.

6

Form the dough into small balls with floured
hands. Add the cider vinegar to the meat and
spoon the dumplings on top. Cook for a
further 20 minutes, until the dumplings
have cooked through, and serve hot.

Steak and Kidney Pie, with Mustard and Bay Gravy

*This is a sharpened-up, bay-flavoured version of a traditional favourite. The fragrant
mustard, bay and parsley perfectly complement the flavour of the beef.*

INGREDIENTS

450 g / 1 lb puff pastry
2½ tbsp flour
salt and pepper
750 g / 1½ lb rump steak, cubed
170 g / 6 oz pig's or lamb's kidney
25 g / 1 oz / scant 2 tbsp butter
1 medium onion, chopped
1 tbsp made English mustard
2 bay leaves
1 tbsp chopped parsley
150 ml / 5 fl oz beef stock
1 egg, beaten

Serves 4

1

Roll out two-thirds of the pastry on a
floured surface to about 3 mm / ⅛ in thick.
Line a 1.5 litre / 2½ pint pie dish. Place a
pie funnel in the middle.

2

Put the flour, salt and pepper in a bowl and
toss the cubes of steak in the mixture.
Remove all fat and skin from the kidneys,
and slice thickly. Add to the steak cubes
and toss well. Melt the butter in a pan and
fry the chopped onion until soft, then add
the mustard, bay leaves, parsley and stock
and stir well.

3

Preheat the oven to 190°C / 375°F / Gas
Mark 5. Place the steak and kidney in the
pie and add the stock mixture. Roll out the
remaining pastry to a thickness of
3 mm / ⅛ in. Brush the edges of the pastry
forming the lower half of the pie with
beaten egg and cover with the second piece
of pastry. Press the pieces of pastry together
to seal the edges, then trim. Use the
trimmings to decorate the top with a
pattern of leaves.

4

Brush the whole pie with beaten egg and
make a small hole over the top of the
funnel. Bake for about 1 hour until the
pastry is golden brown.

Veal Kidneys with Mustard

This dish is equally delicious made with lamb's kidneys. Be sure not to cook the sauce too long after adding the mustard or it will lose its piquancy.

INGREDIENTS

*2 veal kidneys or 8–10 lamb's
kidneys, skinned
25 g / 1 oz / 2 tbsp butter
15 ml / 1 tbsp vegetable oil
115 g / 4 oz / 1 cup button
mushrooms, quartered
60 ml / 4 tbsp chicken stock
30 ml / 2 tbsp brandy (optional)
175 ml / 6 fl oz / ¾ cup crème fraîche
or double cream
30 ml / 2 tbsp Dijon mustard
salt and freshly ground black pepper
snipped fresh chives, to garnish*

Serves 4

3

Add the mushrooms to the pan and sauté for 2–3 minutes until golden, stirring frequently. Pour in the chicken stock and brandy, if using, then bring to the boil and boil for 2 minutes.

4

Stir in the cream and cook for about 2–3 minutes until the sauce is slightly thickened. Stir in the mustard and seasoning, then add the kidneys and cook for 1 minute. Scatter over the chives before serving.

1

Cut the kidneys into pieces, discarding any fat. If using lamb's kidneys, remove the central core by cutting a V-shape from the middle of each kidney. Cut each kidney into three or four pieces.

2

Melt the butter with the oil in a large frying pan. Add the kidneys, sauté over a high heat for about 3–4 minutes, stirring frequently, until well browned, then transfer them to a plate using a slotted spoon.

White Veal Stew

In France, this farmhouse stew is known as a blanquette because it is enriched with cream, giving it a white colour. It is traditionally made with veal, but can be made with lamb.

INGREDIENTS

1.5 kg / 3–3½ lb boneless veal shoulder, cut into 5 cm / 2 in cubes
1.5 litres / 2½ pints / 6 cups veal or chicken stock
1 large onion, studded with 2 cloves
4 carrots, sliced
2 leeks, sliced
1 garlic clove, halved
1 bouquet garni
15 ml / 1 tbsp black peppercorns
65 g / 2½ oz / 5 tbsp butter
225 g / 8 oz / 2 cups button mushrooms, quartered if large
225 g / 8 oz / 1½ cups shallots or baby onions
15 ml / 1 tbsp caster sugar
40 g / 1½ oz / ⅓ cup plain flour
120ml / 4 fl oz / ½ cup crème fraîche or double cream
pinch of grated nutmeg
60 ml / 4 tbsp chopped fresh dill or parsley
salt and white pepper
fresh herb sprigs, to garnish

Serves 6

1

Put the veal and stock in a large, flameproof casserole. Bring to the boil, skim the surface, then add the studded onion, one of the sliced carrots, the leeks, garlic, bouquet garni and peppercorns. Cover, lower the heat and simmer for about 1 hour until the veal is just tender.

2

Meanwhile melt 15 g / ½ oz / 1 tbsp of the butter in a frying pan and sauté the mushrooms until lightly golden. Transfer to a large bowl, using a slotted spoon.

3

Melt another 15 g / ½ oz / 1 tbsp of the butter in the pan and add the shallots or onions. Sprinkle with the sugar and add about 90 ml / 6 tbsp of the veal cooking liquid. Cover and simmer for 10–12 minutes until the onions are tender and the liquid has evaporated. Add the onions to the mushrooms.

4

When the veal is tender, transfer the cubes to the bowl of vegetables using a slotted spoon. Strain the veal cooking liquid and discard the cooked vegetables and bouquet garni, then wash the casserole and return it to the heat.

5

Melt the remaining butter, add the flour and cook for 1–2 minutes. Gradually whisk in the reserved cooking liquid. Bring to the boil, then lower the heat and simmer the sauce until smooth and slightly thickened. Add the remaining carrots and cook for a further 10 minutes until tender.

6

Whisk the cream into the sauce and simmer until slightly thickened. Add the meat, mushrooms and onions and simmer for 10–15 minutes until the veal is very tender. Season with salt, white pepper and a little nutmeg, then stir in the chopped dill or parsley. Garnish with fresh herb sprigs and serve.

Puddings

When it comes to puddings, farmhouse cooks are fortunate. They may need to go no further than the orchard to pick scented apples, pears or bright red cherries. Sticks of rhubarb, sweet soft fruits and juicy plums are there for the taking. No wonder their puddings are so delicious. The following pages offer an abundance of ideas to serve as a final course for anything from a family meal to a formal dinner party. Serve them with dollops of thick cream or lashings of rich custard for an extra special treat.

Lemon Meringue Bombe with Mint Chocolate

This easy ice cream will cause a sensation at a dinner party – it is unusual but quite the
most delicious combination of tastes that you can imagine.

INGREDIENTS

2 large lemons
150 g / 5 oz granulated sugar
3 small sprigs fresh mint
150 ml / ¼ pint whipping cream
600 ml / 1 pint natural yogurt
2 large meringues
225 g / 8 oz good-quality mint
chocolate, grated

Serves 6–8

1

Slice the rind off the lemons with a potato peeler, then squeeze them for juice. Place the lemon rind and sugar in a food processor and blend finely. Add the cream, yogurt and lemon juice and process thoroughly. Pour the mixture into a mixing bowl and add the meringues, roughly crushed.

3

When the ice cream has frozen, scoop out the middle and pour in the grated mint chocolate. Replace the ice cream to cover the chocolate and refreeze.

2

Reserve one of the mint sprigs and chop the rest finely. Add to the mixture. Pour into a 1.2 litre / 2 pint glass bowl and freeze for 4 hours.

4

To turn out, dip the basin in very hot water for a few seconds to loosen the ice cream, then turn the basin upside down over the serving plate. Decorate with grated chocolate and a sprig of mint.

Apple Mint and Pink Grapefruit Fool

*Apple mint can easily run riot in the herb garden; this is an excellent
way of using up an abundant crop.*

*500 g / 1 lb tart apples, peeled, cored
and sliced*
225 g / 8 oz pink grapefruit segments
45 ml / 3 tbsp clear honey
30 ml / 2 tbsp water
*6 large sprigs apple mint, plus more
to garnish*
150 ml / ¼ pint double cream
300 ml / ½ pint custard

Serves 4–6

1

Place the apples, grapefruit, honey, water
and apple mint in a pan, cover and simmer
for 10 minutes until soft. Leave in the pan
to cool, then discard the apple mint. Purée
the mixture in a food processor.

2

Whip the cream until it forms soft peaks,
and fold into the custard, keeping 2 tbsp to
decorate. Carefully fold the cream into the
fruit mixture. Serve chilled and decorated
with swirls of cream and sprigs of mint.

Country Strawberry Fool

*Make this delicious fool on the day you want to eat it, and chill it well,
for the best strawberry taste.*

INGREDIENTS

300 ml / ½ pint / 1¼ cups milk
2 egg yolks
90 g / 3½ oz / scant ½ cup
caster sugar
few drops of vanilla essence
900 g / 2 lb ripe strawberries
juice of ½ lemon
300 ml / ½ pint / 1¼ cups double
cream

To decorate
12 small strawberries
4 fresh mint sprigs

Serves 4

1

First make the custard. Whisk 30 ml / 2 tbsp milk with the egg yolks, 15 ml / 1 tbsp caster sugar and the vanilla essence.

2

Heat the remaining milk until it is just below boiling point.

3

Stir the milk into the egg mixture. Rinse the pan out and return the mixture to it.

4

Gently heat and whisk until the mixture thickens (it should be thick enough to coat the back of a spoon). Lay a wet piece of greaseproof paper on top of the custard and leave it to cool.

5

Purée the strawberries in a food processor or blender with the lemon juice and the remaining sugar.

6

Lightly whip the cream and fold in the fruit purée and custard. Pour into glass dishes and decorate with the whole strawberries and sprigs of mint.

Orange-blossom Jelly

A fresh orange jelly makes a delightful dessert: the natural fruit flavour combined with the smooth jelly has a cleansing quality that is especially welcome after a rich main course. This is delicious served with thin, crisp langues de chat *biscuits.*

INGREDIENTS

65 g / 2½ oz / 5 tbsp caster sugar
150 ml / ¼ pint / ⅔ cup water
2 sachets of gelatine
(about 25 g / 1 oz)
600 ml / 1 pint / 2½ cups freshly
squeezed orange juice
30 ml / 2 tbsp orange-flower water

Serves 4–6

1

Place the caster sugar and water in a small saucepan and gently heat to dissolve the sugar. Leave to cool.

2

Sprinkle over the gelatine, ensuring it is completely submerged in the water. Leave to stand until the gelatine has absorbed all the liquid and is solid.

3

Gently melt the gelatine over a bowl of simmering water until it becomes clear and transparent. Leave to cool. When the gelatine is cold, mix it with the orange juice and orange-flower water.

4

Wet a jelly mould and pour in the jelly. Chill in the refrigerator for at least 2 hours, or until set. Turn out to serve.

Steamed Ginger and Cinnamon Syrup Pudding

A traditional and comforting steamed pudding, best served with custard.

INGREDIENTS

120 g / 4½ oz / 9 tbsp softened
butter
45 ml / 3 tbsp golden syrup
115 g / 4 oz / ½ cup caster sugar
2 eggs, lightly beaten
115 g / 4 oz / 1 cup plain flour
5 ml / 1 tsp baking powder
5 ml / 1 tsp ground cinnamon
25 g / 1 oz stem ginger,
finely chopped
30 ml / 2 tbsp milk

Serves 4

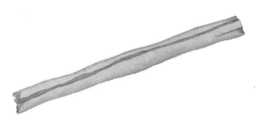

1

Set a full steamer or saucepan of water on to boil. Lightly grease a 600 ml / 1 pint / 2½ cup pudding basin with 15 g / ½ oz / 1 tbsp butter. Place the golden syrup in the basin.

2

Cream the remaining butter and sugar together until light and fluffy. Gradually add the eggs until the mixture is glossy. Sift the flour, baking powder and cinnamon together and fold them into the mixture, with the stem ginger. Add the milk to make a soft, dropping consistency.

3

Spoon the batter into the basin and smooth the top. Cover with a pleated piece of greaseproof paper, to allow for expansion during cooking. Tie securely with string and steam for 1½–2 hours, making sure that the water level is kept topped up, to ensure a good flow of steam to cook the pudding. Turn the pudding out to serve it.

Poached Pears

Serve warm with clotted cream and crisp shortbread fingers.

INGREDIENTS

6 medium pears
350 g / 12 oz / 1¾ cups caster
sugar
75 ml / 5 tbsp runny honey
1 vanilla pod
600 ml / 1 pint / 2½ cups red wine
5 ml / 1 tsp whole cloves
7 cm / 3 in cinnamon stick

Serves 4

1

Peel the pears but leave them whole,
keeping the stalks as well.

2

Put the sugar, honey, vanilla pod, wine,
cloves and cinnamon stick in a large pan.

3

Add the pears and poach until soft, about
30 minutes. When the pears are tender,
remove them with a slotted spoon and keep
them warm. Remove the vanilla pod, cloves
and cinnamon stick and boil the liquid
until it is reduced by half. Serve spooned
over the pears.

Cherry Clafoutis

This is a traditional French Farmhouse way of serving fresh cherries.

INGREDIENTS

675 g / 1½ lb / 6 cups fresh cherries
50 g / 2oz / ½ cup plain flour
pinch of salt
4 eggs, plus 2 egg yolks
115 g / 4oz / ½ cup caster sugar, plus
extra for dusting
600 ml / 1 pint / 2½ cups milk
50 g / 2 oz / ¼ cup melted butter, plus
extra for greasing

Serves 6

1

Preheat the oven to 190°C / 375°F / Gas
Mark 5. Lightly butter the base and sides of
a shallow ovenproof dish. Stone the cherries
and place them in a single layer in the dish.

2

Sift the flour and salt into a bowl. Add the
eggs, egg yolks, sugar and a little of the
milk and whisk to a smooth batter.

3

Gradually whisk in the rest of the milk and
the melted butter, then strain the batter
over the cherries. Bake for 40–50 minutes
until golden and just set. Serve warm,
dusted with caster sugar.

NOTE

If fresh cherries are not available use two
425 g / 15 oz cans stoned black cherries,
thoroughly drained. For a special dessert,
add 45 ml / 3 tbsp Kirsch or cherry brandy
to the batter.

Mint Ice Cream

This ice cream is best served slightly softened, so take it out
of the freezer 20 minutes before you want to serve it. For a special occasion,
this looks spectacular served in an ice bowl.

INGREDIENTS

8 egg yolks
75 g / 3 oz / 6 tbsp caster sugar
600 ml / 1 pint / 2½ cups single
cream
1 vanilla pod
60 ml / 4 tbsp chopped fresh mint

Serves 8

1

Beat the egg yolks and sugar until they are
pale and light using a hand-held electric
beater or a balloon whisk. Transfer to a
small saucepan.

2

In a separate saucepan, bring the cream to
the boil with the vanilla pod.

3

Remove the vanilla pod and pour the hot cream
on to the egg mixture, whisking briskly.

4

Continue whisking to ensure the eggs
are mixed into the cream.

5

Gently heat the mixture until the custard
thickens enough to coat the back of a
wooden spoon. Leave to cool.

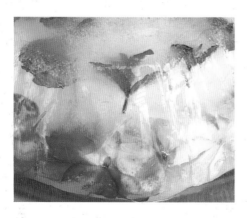

6

Stir in the mint and place in an ice-cream
maker to churn, about 3–4 hours. If you
don't have an ice-cream maker, freeze the
ice cream until mushy and then whisk it well
again, to break down the ice crystals. Freeze
for another 3 hours until it is softly frozen
and whisk again. Finally freeze until hard:
at least 6 hours.

Summer Fruit Gâteau with Heartsease

No one could resist the appeal of little heartsease pansies. This cake would be lovely for a sentimental summer occasion in the garden.

INGREDIENTS

100 g / 3½ oz / scant ½ cup soft
margarine, plus more to grease mould
100 g / 3¾ oz / scant ½ cup sugar
10 ml / 2 tsp clear honey
150 g / 5 oz / 1¼ cups self-raising flour
3 ml / ½ tsp baking powder
30 ml / 2 tbsp milk
2 eggs, plus white of one more for
crystallizing
15 ml / 1 tbsp rosewater
15 ml / 1 tbsp Cointreau
16 heartsease flowers
caster sugar, as required, to crystallize
icing sugar, to decorate
500 g / 1 lb strawberries
strawberry leaves, to decorate

Serves 6–8

1

Crystallize the heartsease pansies by painting them with lightly beaten egg white and sprinkling with caster sugar. Leave to dry.

2

Preheat the oven to 190°C/375°F/ Gas Mark 5. Grease and lightly flour a ring mould.

3

Take a large mixing bowl and add the soft margarine, sugar, honey, flour, baking powder, milk and 2 eggs to the mixing bowl and beat well for 1 minute. Add the rosewater and the Cointreau and mix well.

4

Pour the mixture into the pan and bake for 40 minutes. Allow to stand for a few minutes and then turn out on to the plate that you wish to serve it on.

5

Sift icing sugar over the cake. Fill the centre of the ring with strawberries. Decorate with crystallized heartsease flowers and some strawberry leaves.

Borage, Mint and Lemon Balm Sorbet

Borage has such a pretty flower head that it is worth growing just to make this recipe, and to float the flowers in summer drinks. The sorbet itself has a very refreshing, delicate taste, perfect for a hot afternoon.

INGREDIENTS

500 g / 1 lb / 2⅛ cups sugar
500 ml / 17 fl oz / 2⅛ cups water
6 sprigs mint, plus more to decorate
6 lemon balm leaves
250 ml / 8 fl oz / 1 cup white wine
30 ml / 2 tbsp lemon juice
borage sprigs, to decorate

Serves 6–8

1

Place the sugar and water in a saucepan with the washed herbs. Bring to a boil. Remove from the heat and add the wine. Cover and cool. Chill for several hours, then add the lemon juice. Freeze and as soon as the mixture begins to freeze, stir briskly and replace in the freezer. Repeat every 15 minutes for at least 3 hours.

3

Place a small freezer-proof bowl inside each larger bowl and put inside a heavy weight such as a metal weight from some scales. Fill with more cooled boiled water, float more herbs in this and freeze.

2

To make the small ice bowls, pour about 1 cm / ½ in cold, boiled water into small freezer-proof bowls about 600 ml / 1 pint/1¼ US pints in capacity, and arrange some herbs in the water. Freeze, then add a little more water to cover the herbs.

4

To release the ice bowls, warm the inner bowl with a small amount of very hot water and twist it out. Warm the outer bowl by standing it in very hot water for a few seconds then tip out the ice bowl. Spoon the sorbet into the ice bowls and decorate with sprigs of mint and borage.

Blackberry Charlotte

A classic pudding, perfect for cold days. Serve with lightly whipped cream or home-made custard.

INGREDIENTS

65 g / 2½ oz / 5 tbsp unsalted butter
175 g / 6 oz / 3 cups fresh white breadcrumbs
50 g / 2 oz / 4 tbsp soft brown sugar
60 ml / 4 tbsp golden syrup
finely grated rind and juice of 2 lemons
50 g / 2 oz walnut halves
450 g / 1 lb blackberries
450 g / 1 lb cooking apples, peeled, cored and finely sliced

Serves 4

1

Preheat the oven to 180°C / 350°F / Gas Mark 4. Grease a 450 ml / ¾ pint / 2 cup dish with 15 g / ½ oz / 1 tbsp of the butter. Melt the remaining butter and add the breadcrumbs. Sauté them for 5–7 minutes, until the crumbs are a little crisp and golden. Leave to cool slightly.

2

Place the sugar, syrup, lemon rind and juice in a small saucepan and gently warm them. Add the crumbs.

3

Process the walnuts until they are finely ground.

4

Arrange a thin layer of blackberries on the dish. Top with a thin layer of crumbs.

5

Add a thin layer of apple, topping it with another thin layer of crumbs. Repeat the process with another layer of blackberries, followed by a layer of crumbs. Continue until you have used up all the ingredients, finishing with a layer of crumbs.

The mixture should be piled well above the top edge of the dish, because it shrinks during cooking. Bake for 30 minutes, until the crumbs are golden and the fruit is soft.

Mixed Berry Tart

The orange-flavoured pastry is delicious with the fresh fruits of summer.
Serve this with some extra shreds of orange rind scattered on top.

INGREDIENTS

For the pastry
225 g / 8 oz / 2 cups plain flour
115 g / 4 oz / ½ cup unsalted
butter
finely grated rind of 1 orange,
plus extra to decorate

For the filling
300 ml / ½ pint / 1¼ cups
crème fraîche
finely grated rind of 1 lemon
10 ml / 2 tsp icing sugar
675 g / 1½ lb mixed
summer berries

Serves 8

1

To make the pastry, put the flour and butter in a large bowl. Rub in the butter until the mixture resembles breadcrumbs.

2

Add the orange rind and enough cold water to make a soft dough.

3

Roll into a ball and chill for at least 30 minutes. Roll out the pastry on a lightly floured surface.

4

Line a 23 cm / 9 in loose-based flan tin with the pastry. Chill for 30 minutes. Preheat the oven to 200°C / 400°F / Gas Mark 6 and place a baking sheet in the oven to heat up. Line the tin with greaseproof paper and baking beans and bake blind on the baking sheet for 15 minutes. Remove the paper and beans and bake for 10 minutes more, until the pastry is golden. Allow to cool completely. To make the filling, whisk the crème fraîche, lemon rind and sugar together and pour into the pastry case. Top with fruit, sprinkle with orange rind and serve sliced.

French Apple Tart

For added flavour, scatter some toasted, flaked almonds over the top of this classic tart.

INGREDIENTS

For the pastry
115 g / 4 oz / ½ cup unsalted
butter, softened
50 g / 2 oz / 4 tbsp vanilla sugar
1 egg
225 g / 8 oz / 2 cups plain flour

For the filling
50 g / 2 oz / 4 tbsp unsalted butter
5 large tart apples, peeled, cored
and sliced
juice of ½ lemon
300 ml / ½ pint / 1¼ cups double
cream
2 egg yolks
25 g / 1 oz / 2 tbsp vanilla sugar
50 g / 2 oz / ⅔ cup ground
almonds, toasted
25 g / 1 oz / 2 tbsp flaked almonds,
toasted, to garnish

Serves 8

1

Place the butter and sugar in a food processor
and process them well together. Add the egg
and process to mix it in well.

2

Add the flour and process till you have a
soft dough. Wrap the dough in cling film
and chill it for 30 minutes.

3

Roll the pastry out on a lightly floured
surface to about 22–25 cm / 9–10 in diameter.

4

Line a flan tin with the pastry and chill it
for a further 30 minutes. Preheat the oven
to 220°C / 425°F / Gas Mark 7 and place a
baking sheet in the oven to heat up. Line the
pastry case with greaseproof paper and
baking beans and bake blind on the baking
sheet for 10 minutes. Then remove the beans
and paper and cook for a further 5 minutes.

5

Turn the oven down to 190°C / 375°F /
Gas Mark 5. To make the filling, melt the
butter in a frying pan and lightly sauté the
apples for 5–7 minutes. Sprinkle the apples
with lemon juice.

6

Beat the cream and egg yolks with the sugar.
Stir in the toasted ground almonds. Arrange
the apple slices on top of the warm pastry
and pour over the cream mixture. Bake for
25 minutes, or until the cream is just about
set — it tastes better if the cream is still
slightly runny in the centre. Serve hot or cold,
scattered with flaked almonds.

Spiced Red Fruit Compote

When summer fruits are at their best, what could be nicer than a simple compote?

INGREDIENTS

4 ripe red plums, halved
225 g / 8 oz / 2 cups strawberries,
halved
225 g / 8 oz / 1¾ cups raspberries
30 ml / 2 tbsp light muscovado sugar
30 ml / 2 tbsp cold water
1 cinnamon stick
3 pieces of star anise
6 cloves
natural yogurt or fromage frais, to
serve

Serves 4

1

Place all the ingredients, except the yogurt or fromage frais, in a heavy-based pan. Heat gently, without boiling, until the sugar dissolves and the fruit juices run.

2

Cover the pan and leave the fruit to infuse over a very low heat for about 5 minutes. Remove the spices from the compote before serving warm with natural yogurt or fromage frais.

Rhubarb Spiral Cobbler

Typical farmhouse fare: stewed rhubarb with spiral scone topping.

INGREDIENTS

675 g / 1½ lb rhubarb, sliced
45 ml / 3 tbsp orange juice
75 g / 3 oz / 6 tbsp caster sugar
200 g / 7 oz / 1¾ cups self-raising flour
250 ml / 8 fl oz / 1 cup natural yogurt
grated rind of 1 medium orange
30 ml / 2 tbsp demerara sugar
5 ml / 1 tsp ground ginger
Greek-style yogurt or custard, to serve

Serves 4

1

Preheat the oven to 200°C / 400°F / Gas Mark 6. Cook the rhubarb with the orange juice and two-thirds of the sugar until tender. Transfer to an ovenproof dish.

2

To make the topping, mix the flour with the remaining caster sugar, then gradually stir in enough of the yogurt to bind to a soft dough.

3

Roll out the dough on a floured surface to a 25 cm / 10 in square. Mix the orange rind, demerara sugar and ginger, then sprinkle this over the dough.

4

Roll up the dough quite tightly, then cut into about 10 slices. Arrange the dough slices over the rhubarb.

5

Bake the cobbler for 15–20 minutes, or until the spirals are well risen and golden brown. Serve warm with Greek-style yogurt or custard.

Rhubarb and Orange Crumble

The almonds give this crumble topping a nutty taste and crunchy texture.
This crumble is extra-delicious with home-made custard.

INGREDIENTS

900 g / 2 lb rhubarb, cut in
5 cm / 2 in lengths
75 g / 3 oz / 6 tbsp caster sugar
finely grated rind and juice
of 2 oranges

115 g / 4 oz / 1 cup plain flour
115 g / 4 oz / ½ cup unsalted
butter, chilled and cubed
75 g / 3 oz / 6 tbsp demerara sugar
115 g / 4 oz / 1¼ cups ground almonds

Serves 6

1

Preheat the oven to 180°C / 350°F /
Gas Mark 4. Place the rhubarb in a shallow
ovenproof dish.

2

Sprinkle over the caster sugar and add the
orange rind and juice.

3

Sift the flour into a mixing bowl and add the
butter. Rub the butter into the flour until
the mixture resembles breadcrumbs.

4

Add the demerara sugar and ground almonds
and mix well.

5

Spoon the crumble mixture over the fruit to
cover it completely. Bake for 40 minutes,
until the top is browned and the fruit is
cooked. Serve warm.

Christmas Pudding

The classic Christmas dessert. Wrap it in muslin and store it in an airtight container for up to a year for the flavours to develop.

INGREDIENTS

115 g / 4 oz / 1 cup plain flour
pinch of salt
5 ml / 1 tsp ground mixed spice
¹/₂ tsp ground cinnamon
¹/₄ tsp freshly grated nutmeg
225 g / 8 oz / 1 cup grated hard white fat
1 dessert apple, grated
225 g / 8 oz / 2 cups fresh white breadcrumbs
350 g / 12 oz / 1⁷/₈ cups soft brown sugar
50 g / 2 oz flaked almonds
225 g / 8 oz / 1¹/₂ cups seedless raisins
225 g / 8 oz / 1¹/₂ cups currants
225 g / 8 oz / 1¹/₂ cups sultanas
115 g / 4 oz ready-to-eat dried apricots
115 g / 4 oz / ³/₄ cup chopped mixed peel
finely grated rind and juice of 1 lemon
30 ml / 2 tbsp black treacle
3 eggs
300 ml / ¹/₂ pint / 1¹/₄ cups milk
30 ml / 2 tbsp rum

Serves 8

1

Sieve the flour, salt and spices into a large bowl.

2

Add the fat, apple and other dry ingredients, including the grated lemon rind.

3

Heat the treacle until warm and runny and pour into the dry ingredients.

4

Mix together the eggs, milk, rum and lemon juice.

5

Stir the liquid into the dry mixture.

6

Spoon the mixture into two 1.2 litre / 2 pint / 5 cup basins. Overwrap the puddings with pieces of greaseproof paper, pleated to allow for expansion, and tie with string. Steam the puddings in a steamer or saucepan of boiling water. Each pudding needs 10 hours' cooking and 3 hours' reheating. Remember to keep the water level topped up to keep the pans from boiling dry. Serve decorated with holly.

Baking

When the aroma of newly baked bread and cakes is in the air, everyone makes a beeline for the farmhouse kitchen. The kettle has just boiled and there's Irish soda bread or cheese scones for tea, together with butter biscuits, dark fruit cake and a marvellous maple walnut pie. The anticipation of feasting on these delights is almost as enjoyable as the eating. The following section provides a selection of traditional breads, cakes, tarts and other bakes that will be enjoyed by all the family time and time again.

Harvest Loaf

The centrepiece for celebrations when the harvest is safely gathered in, the harvest loaf is a potent symbol of country life. It is too salty to eat, but looks wonderful. It is traditionally displayed at the altar amongst the fruit and vegetables and other offerings from the people of the parish. Although there were many different designs of harvest loaf, the most enduringly popular was the wheatsheaf, symbolic as it is of the harvest and the vital importance of bread as "the staff of life".

INGREDIENTS

1.5kg / 3½ lb / 14 cups strong white flour
30 ml / 2 tbsp salt
2 x 10g / ¼ oz sachets easy-blend dried yeast
750–900 ml / 1¼–1½ pints / 3–3¾ cups hand-hot water
beaten eggs, to glaze

Makes 2 x 800g / 1¾ lb loaves

1

Sift the flour and salt into a large mixing bowl and stir in the yeast. Add enough hand-hot water to make a rough dough. Knead on a lightly floured surface for about 10 minutes, until smooth and elastic. Place the dough in a lightly oiled bowl, cover and leave to prove for 1–2 hours, until it has doubled in bulk.

2

Preheat the oven to 220°C / 425°F / Gas Mark 7. Oil and flour a large baking sheet. Roll out about 225 g / 8 oz of the dough into a 30 cm / 12 in long cylinder. Place it on the baking sheet and flatten slightly with your hand. This will form the body of the bread, symbolizing the long stalks of the wheatsheaf. The high salt content in the dough makes it easier to work, but the bread is more decorative than palatable.

3

Roll and shape about 350 g / 12 oz of the remaining dough into a crescent; place this at the top of the cylinder and flatten. Divide the remaining dough in half. Take one half and divide it in two again. Use one half to make the stalks of the wheat by rolling into narrow ropes and placing on the "stalk" of the sheaf. Use the other half to make a plait to decorate the finished loaf where the stalks meet the ears of wheat.

4

Use the remaining dough to make the ears of wheat. Roll it into small sausage shapes and snip each a few times with scissors to give the effect of the separate ears. Place these on the crescent shape, fanning out from the base until the wheatsheaf is complete. Position the plait between the stalks and the ears of wheat. Brush the wheatsheaf with the beaten egg. Bake for 20 minutes, then reduce the heat to 160°C / 325°F / Gas Mark 3 and bake for 20 minutes more.

Olive Bread

Olive breads are popular all over the Mediterranean. For this Greek recipe use rich, oily olives or those marinated in herbs rather than canned ones.

INGREDIENTS

2 red onions
30 ml / 2 tbsp olive oil
225 g / 8 oz / 1⅓ cups pitted black or green olives
800 g / 1¾ lb / 7 cups strong white flour
7.5 ml / 1½ tsp salt
20 ml / 4 tsp easy-blend dried yeast
45 ml / 3 tbsp roughly chopped fresh parsley, coriander or mint
475 ml / 16 fl oz / 2 cups hand-hot water

Makes 2 x 675g / 1½ lb loaves

VARIATION

Shape the dough into 16 small rolls. Slash the tops as below and reduce the cooking time to 25 minutes.

1

Slice the onions thinly. Fry them gently in the oil until soft. Roughly chop the olives.

2

Put the flour, salt, yeast and parsley, coriander or mint in a large bowl. Stir in the olives and fried onions, then pour in the hand-hot water. Mix to a dough, adding a little more water if the mixture feels dry.

3

Knead on a lightly floured surface for about 10 minutes, until smooth and elastic. Cut the dough in half. Shape into two rounds and place on two oiled baking sheets. Cover loosely with lightly oiled clear film and leave until doubled in size.

4

Preheat the oven to 220°C / 425°F / Gas Mark 7. Slash the tops of the loaves with a knife. Bake for about 40 minutes or until the loaves sound hollow when tapped on the bottom. Transfer to a wire rack to cool.

Potato Bread

Mashed potatoes make a lovely loaf. Ensure the liquid is only hand-hot when added.

INGREDIENTS

*225 g / 8 oz potatoes, peeled and
halved or quartered
30 ml / 2 tbsp vegetable oil
250 ml / 8 fl oz / 1 cup lukewarm milk
675 g / 1½ lb / 6 cups strong white flour
15 ml / 1 tbsp salt
20 ml / 4 tsp easy-blend dried yeast*

Makes 2 loaves

1

Cook the potatoes in a saucepan of salted
water for 20–30 minutes. Drain and reserve
the cooking water. Return the potatoes to
the pan and mash with oil and milk. Mix
the flour, salt and yeast together. Put the
potato mixture in a bowl. Stir in
250 ml / 8 fl oz / 1 cup of the potato
cooking water, then gradually stir in the
flour mixture to form a stiff dough.

2

Knead the dough for 10 minutes. Grease two
23 x 13 cm / 9 x 5 in loaf tins. Roll the
dough into 20 small balls. Place two rows of
balls in each pan. Cover with clear film and
leave in a warm place to rise. Preheat the
oven to 200°C / 400°F / Gas Mark 6. Bake
the loaves for 10 minutes, then lower the
heat to 190°C / 375°F / Gas Mark 5 and
bake for about 40 minutes more.

Irish Soda Bread

This traditional farmhouse loaf needs no rising, so is perfect for unexpected guests.

INGREDIENTS

*225 g / 8 oz / 2 cups plain white
flour, plus extra for dusting
115 g / 4 oz / 1 cup wholemeal flour
5 ml / 1 tsp bicarbonate of soda
5 ml / 1 tsp salt
25 g / 1 oz / 2 tbsp butter, softened
300 ml / ½ pint / 1¼ cups buttermilk*

Makes 1 loaf

1

Preheat the oven to 200°C / 400°F / Gas
Mark 6. Grease a baking sheet. Sift the dry
ingredients into a bowl. Make a well in the
centre and add the butter and buttermilk.
Gradually incorporate the surrounding flour
to make a soft dough. Gather the dough
into a ball. Knead the dough on a floured
surface for 3 minutes. Shape into a round.

2

Place the round on the baking sheet. Cut a
cross in the top with a sharp knife. Dust with
flour, then bake for 40–50 minutes or until
golden brown. Transfer to a rack to cool.

Easter Plait

Serve this delicious plait sliced with butter and jam.
It is also very good toasted on the day after you made it.

INGREDIENTS

200 ml / 7 fl oz / ⁷/₈ cup milk
2 eggs, lightly beaten
450 g / 1 lb / 4 cups plain flour
½ tsp salt
10 ml / 2 tsp ground mixed spice
75 g / 3 oz / 6 tbsp butter
20 g / ¾ oz dried yeast
75 g / 3 oz / 6 tbsp caster sugar

175 g / 6 oz / 1¼ cups currants
25 g / 1 oz / ¼ cup candied mixed peel, chopped
a little sweetened milk, to glaze
25 g / 1 oz / 1½ tbsp glacé cherries, chopped
15 g / ½ oz / 1 tbsp angelica, chopped

Serves 8

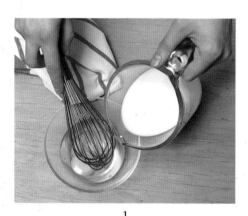

1

Warm the milk to lukewarm, add two-thirds of it to the eggs and mix well.

2

Sift the flour, salt and mixed spice together. Rub in the butter, then add the sugar and dried yeast. Make a well in the centre, and add the milk mixture, adding more milk as necessary to make a sticky dough.

3

Knead on a well-floured surface and then knead in the currants and mixed peel, reserving 15 ml / 1 tbsp for the topping. Put the dough in a lightly greased bowl and cover it with a damp tea towel. Leave to double its size. Preheat the oven to 220°C / 425°F / Gas Mark 7.

4

Turn the dough out on to a floured surface and knead again for 2–3 minutes. Divide the dough into three even pieces. Roll each piece into a sausage shape roughly 20 cm / 8 in long. Plait the three pieces together, turning under and pinching each end. Place on a floured baking sheet and leave to rise for 15 minutes.

5

Brush the top with sweetened milk and scatter with roughly chopped cherries, strips of angelica and the reserved mixed peel. Bake in the preheated oven for 45 minutes or until the bread sounds hollow when tapped on the bottom. Cool slightly on a wire rack.

Wholemeal Bread

Home-made bread creates one of the most evocative smells in country cooking.
Eat this on the day of making, to enjoy the superb fresh taste.

INGREDIENTS

20 g / ¾ oz fresh yeast
300 ml / ½ pint / 1¼ cups
lukewarm milk
5 ml / 1 tsp caster sugar
225 g / 8 oz / 1½ cups strong
wholemeal flour, sifted
225 g / 8 oz / 2 cups strong
white flour, sifted
5 ml / 1 tsp salt
50 g / 2 oz / 4 tbsp butter,
chilled and cubed
1 egg, lightly beaten
30 ml / 2 tbsp mixed seeds

Makes 4 rounds or 2 loaves

1

Gently dissolve the yeast with a little of the milk and the sugar to make a paste. Place both the flours plus any bran from the sieve and the salt in a large warmed mixing bowl. Rub in the butter until the mixture resembles breadcrumbs.

2

Add the yeast mixture, remaining milk and egg and mix into a fairly soft dough. Knead on a floured board for 15 minutes. Lightly grease the mixing bowl and put the dough back in the bowl, covering it with a piece of greased cling film. Leave to double in size in a warm place (this should take at least an hour).

3

Knock the dough back and knead it for a further 10 minutes. Preheat the oven to 200°C / 400°F / Gas Mark 6. To make round loaves, divide the dough into four pieces and shape them into flattish rounds. Place them on a floured baking sheet and leave to rise for a further 15 minutes. Sprinkle the loaves with the mixed seeds. Bake for about 20 minutes until golden and firm.

NOTE

For tin-shaped loaves, put the knocked-back dough into two greased loaf tins instead. Leave to rise for a further 45 minutes and then bake for about 45 minutes, until the loaf sounds hollow when turned out of the tin and knocked on the base.

Scones

The secret with making scones is not to overwork the dough.

225 g / 8 oz / 2 cups plain flour
5 ml / 1 tsp baking powder
½ tsp bicarbonate of soda
5 ml / 1 tsp salt
50 g / 2 oz / ¼ cup butter or
margarine, chilled
175 ml / 6 fl oz / ¾ cup buttermilk or
soured milk

Makes 10

1

Preheat the oven to 220°C / 425°F / Gas
Mark 7. Sift the dry ingredients into a
mixing bowl. Mix in the butter or
margarine with a fork until the mixture
resembles coarse breadcrumbs.

2

Add the buttermilk or soured milk and
mix swiftly to a soft dough.

3

Knead the dough on a lightly floured board
for 30 seconds.

4

Roll or pat out the dough to a thickness of
1 cm / ½ in. Use a floured 6 cm / 2½ in
pastry cutter to cut out 10 rounds. Transfer
the rounds to a baking sheet and bake for
10–12 minutes, until well risen and golden
brown.

Cheese Scones

These delicious scones make a good tea-time treat. They are best served fresh and still slightly warm.

INGREDIENTS

225 g / 8 oz / 2 cups plain flour
12 ml / 2½ tsp baking powder
½ tsp dry mustard powder
½ tsp salt
50 g / 2 oz / 4 tbsp butter, chilled
75 g / 3 oz Cheddar cheese, grated
150 ml / ¼ pint / ⅔ cup milk
1 egg, beaten

Makes 12

1

Preheat the oven to 230°C / 450°F / Gas Mark 8. Sift the flour, baking powder, mustard powder and salt into a mixing bowl. Add the butter and rub it into the flour mixture until the mixture resembles breadcrumbs. Stir in 50 g / 2 oz of the cheese.

2

Make a well in the centre and add the milk and egg. Mix gently and then turn the dough out on to a lightly floured surface. Roll it out and cut it into triangles or squares. Brush lightly with milk and sprinkle with the remaining cheese. Leave to rest for 15 minutes, then bake them for 15 minutes, or until well risen.

Oatcakes

These are very simple to make and are an excellent addition to a cheese board.

INGREDIENTS

225 g / 8 oz / 1⅔ cups medium oatmeal
75 g / 3 oz / ¾ cup plain flour
¼ tsp bicarbonate of soda
5 ml / 1 tsp salt
25 g / 1 oz / 2 tbsp hard white vegetable fat
25 g / 1 oz / 2 tbsp butter

Makes 24

1

Preheat the oven to 220°C / 425°F / Gas Mark 7. Place the oatmeal, flour, soda and salt in a large bowl. Gently melt the two fats together in a pan.

2

Add the melted fat and enough boiling water to make a soft dough. Turn out on to a surface scattered with a little oatmeal. Roll out the dough thinly and cut it into circles. Bake the oatcakes on ungreased baking trays for 15 minutes, until crisp.

Cranberry Muffins

A tea or breakfast dish that is not too sweet.

INGREDIENTS

350 g / 12 oz / 3 cups plain flour
15 ml / 1 tsp baking powder
pinch of salt
115 g / 4 oz / ½ cup caster sugar
2 eggs
150 ml / ¼ pint / ⅔ cup milk
50 ml / 2 fl oz / 4 tbsp corn oil
finely grated rind of 1 orange
150 g / 5 oz cranberries

Makes 12

1

Preheat the oven to 190°C / 375°F /
Gas Mark 5. Line 12 deep muffin tins with
paper cases. Mix the flour, baking powder,
salt and caster sugar together.

2

Lightly beat the eggs with the milk and oil.
Add them to the dry ingredients and blend
to make a smooth batter. Stir in the orange
rind and cranberries. Divide the mixture
between the muffin cases and bake for
25 minutes until risen and golden.
Leave to cool in the tins for a few minutes,
and serve warm or cold.

Scotch Pancakes

Serve these while still warm, with butter and jam.

INGREDIENTS

*225 g / 8 oz / 2 cups self-raising
flour*
50 g / 2 oz / 4 tbsp caster sugar
50 g / 2 oz / 4 tbsp butter, melted
1 egg
300 ml / ½ pint / 1¼ cups milk
15 g / ½ oz / 1 tbsp hard white fat

Makes 24

1

Mix the flour and sugar together. Add the
melted butter and egg with two-thirds of the
milk. Mix to a smooth batter – it should be
thin enough to find its own level.

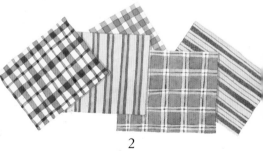

2

Heat a griddle or a heavy-based frying pan
and wipe it with a little hard white fat.
When hot, drop spoonfuls of the mixture
on to the hot griddle or pan. When bubbles
come to the surface of the pancakes, flip them
over to cook until golden on the other side.
Keep the pancakes warm wrapped in a tea
towel while cooking the rest of the mixture.

Butter Biscuits

These little biscuits are similar to shortbread, but richer.
Handle them with care, as they break easily.

INGREDIENTS

200 g / 7 oz / ¾ cup butter, diced,
plus extra for greasing
6 egg yolks, lightly beaten
15 ml / 1 tbsp milk
225 g / 8 oz / 2 cups plain flour
175 g / 6 oz / ¾ cup caster sugar

Makes 18–20

1

Preheat the oven to 180°C / 350°F / Gas Mark 4. Lightly butter a large, heavy baking sheet. Mix 15 ml / 1 tbsp of the beaten egg yolks with the milk, to make a glaze, and set aside.

2

Sift the flour into a large bowl and make a well in the centre. Add the remaining egg yolks, sugar and butter and, using your fingertips, work them together until smooth and creamy.

3

Gradually incorporate the flour to make a smooth, slightly sticky dough.

4

Using floured hands, pat out the dough to a thickness of 8 mm / ⅜ in and cut out rounds using a 7.5 cm / 3 in cutter. Transfer the rounds to a baking sheet, brush each with a little egg glaze, then using the back of a knife, score to create a lattice pattern.

5

Bake for 12–15 minutes until golden. Cool in the tin on a wire rack for 15 minutes, then carefully remove the biscuits and leave to cool completely on the rack.

Orange Shortbread Fingers

*These are a real tea-time treat. The fingers will keep in an airtight tin
for up to two weeks.*

INGREDIENTS

*115 g / 4 oz / ½ cup unsalted
butter, softened
50 g / 2 oz / 4 tbsp caster sugar,
plus a little extra
finely grated rind of 2 oranges
175 g / 6 oz / 1½ cups plain flour*

Makes 18

___
1

Preheat the oven to 190°C / 375°F /
Gas Mark 5. Beat the butter and sugar
together until they are soft and creamy.
Beat in the orange rind.

___
2

Gradually add the flour and gently pull the
dough together to form a soft ball. Roll the
dough out on a lightly floured surface until
about 1 cm / ½ in thick. Cut it into fingers,
sprinkle over a little extra caster sugar,
prick with a fork and bake for about
20 minutes, or until the fingers are a
light golden colour.

Pound Cake

This orange-scented cake is good for tea or as a dessert with a fruit sauce.

INGREDIENTS

*450 g / 1 lb / 3 cups fresh raspberries,
strawberries or stoned cherries, or a
combination of any of these
225 g / 8 oz / 1 cup caster sugar, plus
extra for sprinkling
15 ml / 1 tbsp lemon juice
175 g / 6 oz / 1½ cups plain flour
10 ml / 2 tsp baking powder
pinch of salt
175 g / 6 oz / ¾ cup butter, softened
3 eggs
grated rind of 1 orange
15 ml / 1 tbsp orange juice*

Serves 6–8

1

Reserve a few whole fruits for decorating.
In a food processor fitted with the metal
blade, process the remaining fruit until
smooth. Add 30 ml / 2 tbsp of the sugar
and the lemon juice, then process again to
combine. Strain the sauce and chill.

2

Base-line and grease a 20 x 10 cm / 8 x
4 in loaf tin. Sprinkle the base and sides of
the tin lightly with sugar and tip out any
excess. Preheat the oven to 180°C / 350°F /
Gas Mark 4.

3

Sift the flour with the baking powder and
salt. In a medium bowl, beat the butter
until creamy. Add the remaining sugar and
beat for 4–5 minutes until very light and
fluffy, then add the eggs, one at a time,
beating well after each addition. Beat in the
orange rind and juice.

4

Gently fold in the flour mixture in batches,
then spoon the mixture into the prepared
tin and tap gently to release any air
bubbles. Bake for 35–40 minutes until the
top of the cake is golden and springs back
when touched. Cool in the tin for
10 minutes, then transfer the cake to a wire
rack and cool for 30 minutes more. Remove
the lining paper and serve slices or wedges
of the warm cake with a little of the fruit
sauce. Decorate with the reserved fruit.

Dark Fruit Cake

With its colourful citrus and candied fruit topping, this tasty cake needs no further decoration.

INGREDIENTS

175 g / 6 oz / 1 cup currants
175 g / 6 oz / 1 cup raisins
115 g / 4 oz / ⅔ cup sultanas
50 g / 2 oz / ¼ cup glacé cherries, halved
45 ml / 3 tbsp Madeira or sherry
175 g / 6 oz / ¾ cup butter
175 g / 6 oz / 1 cup dark brown sugar
2 extra large eggs
200 g / 7 oz / 1¾ cups plain flour
10 ml / 2 tsp baking powder
10 ml / 2 tsp each ground ginger,
allspice and cinnamon
15 ml / 1 tbsp molasses
15 ml / 1 tbsp milk
25 g / 1 oz / ¼ cup glacé fruit, chopped
115 g / 4 oz / 1 cup walnuts or pecan
nuts, chopped

For the decoration
225 g / 8 oz / 1 cup granulated sugar
120 ml / 4 fl oz / ½ cup water
1 lemon, thinly sliced
½ orange, thinly sliced
150 g / 5 oz / ½ cup orange marmalade
glacé cherries

Serves 12

1

Mix the currants, raisins, sultanas and cherries in a bowl. Stir in the Madeira or sherry. Cover and leave overnight.

2

Preheat the oven to 150°C / 300°F / Gas Mark 2. Line and grease a 23 cm / 9 in round springform tin. Cream the butter and sugar in a mixing bowl until light and fluffy. Beat in the eggs, one at a time.

3

Sift the flour, baking powder and spices together. Fold into the butter mixture in batches. Fold in the molasses, milk, dried fruit and liquid, glacé fruit and nuts.

4

Spoon into the tin, spreading out so there is a slight hollow in the centre of the mixture. Bake for 2½–3 hours, until a skewer inserted in the cake comes out clean. Cover with foil when the top is golden to prevent over-browning. Cool in the tin on a rack.

5

Mix the sugar and water in a saucepan and bring to the boil. Add the citrus slices and cook for 20 minutes. Remove the fruit with a slotted spoon. Pour the remaining syrup over the cake and leave to cool. Melt the marmalade, then brush over the top of the cake. Decorate with the candied fruit and glacé cherries.

Light Fruit Cake

This is not the conventional fruit cake mixture, but it is moist, rich and absolutely delicious.

INGREDIENTS

*225 g / 8 oz / 1⅓ cups ready-to-eat
prunes
225 g / 8 oz / 1⅓ cups dates
225 g / 8 oz / 1⅓ cups currants
225 g / 8 oz / 1⅓ cups sultanas
250 ml / 8 fl oz / 1 cup dry white wine
250 ml / 8 fl oz / 1 cup rum
350 g / 12 oz / 3 cups plain flour
10 ml / 2 tsp baking powder
5 ml / 1 tsp ground cinnamon
½ tsp grated nutmeg.
225 g / 8 oz / 1 cup butter, at room
temperature
225 g / 8 oz / 1 cup granulated sugar
4 eggs, lightly beaten
5 ml / 1 tsp vanilla essence*

Makes 2 loaves

1

Pit the prunes and dates and chop finely.
Place in a bowl with the currants and
sultanas. Stir in the wine and rum. Cover
and leave to stand for 48 hours. Stir
occasionally.

2

Preheat the oven to 150°C / 300°F / Gas
Mark 2. Line and grease two 23 x 13 cm /
9 x 5 in loaf tins. Sift the flour, baking
powder, cinnamon and nutmeg into a bowl.

3

Cream the butter and sugar together until
light and fluffy. Gradually add the eggs and
vanilla essence. Fold in the flour mixture in
batches, then add the dried fruit mixture
and its liquid. Mix lightly.

4

Divide the mixture between the tins and
bake for about 1½ hours, or until a skewer
inserted in a loaf comes out clean. Cool in
the tin for 20 minutes, then transfer to a
wire rack to cool completely.

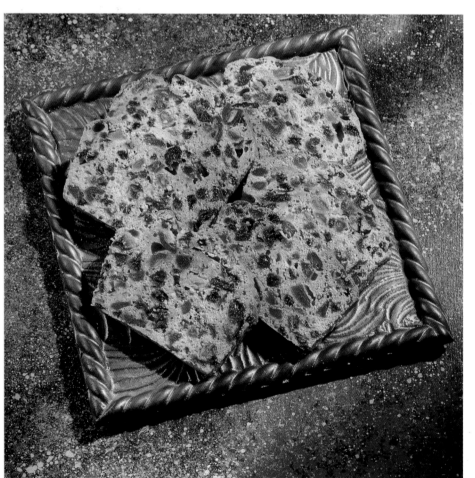

Lemon Drizzle Cake

*You can also make this recipe using a large orange instead of the lemons;
either way, it makes a zesty treat for afternoon tea.*

INGREDIENTS

finely grated rind of 2 lemons
175 g / 6 oz / 12 tbsp caster sugar
*225 g / 8 oz / 1 cup unsalted
butter, softened*
4 eggs
*225 g / 8 oz / 2 cups self-raising
flour*
5 ml / 1 tsp baking powder
¼ tsp salt
*shredded rind of 1 lemon,
to decorate*

For the syrup
juice of 1 lemon
150 g / 5 oz / ¾ cup caster sugar

Serves 6

1

Preheat the oven to 160°C / 325°F /
Gas Mark 3. Grease a 1 kg / 2 lb loaf tin or
18–20 cm / 7–8 in round cake tin and line it
with greaseproof paper or baking parchment.
Mix the lemon rind and caster sugar together.

2

Cream the butter with the lemon and sugar
mixture. Add the eggs and mix until
smooth. Sift the flour, baking powder and
salt into a bowl and fold a third at a time into
the mixture. Turn the batter into the tin,
smooth the top and bake for 1½ hours or
until golden brown and springy to the touch.

3

To make the syrup, slowly heat the juice
with the sugar and dissolve it gently. Make
several slashes in the top of the cake and pour
over the syrup. Sprinkle the shredded lemon
rind and 5 ml / 1 tsp granulated sugar on top
and leave to cool.

Farmhouse Carrot Cake

Marvellously moist and full of flavours, carrot cake has become a true classic.

INGREDIENTS

450 g / 1 lb / 2 cups caster sugar
250 ml / 8 fl oz / 1 cup vegetable oil
4 eggs
about 225 g / 8 oz carrots, finely grated
225 g / 8 oz / 2 cups plain flour
7.5 ml / 1½ tsp bicarbonate of soda
7.5 ml / 1½ tsp baking powder
5 ml / 1 tsp ground allspice
5 ml / 1 tsp ground cinnamon

For the icing
225 g / 8 oz / 2 cups icing sugar
225 / 8 oz / 1 cup cream cheese, softened
50 g / 2 oz / ¼ cup butter, softened
10 ml / 2 tsp vanilla essence
175 g / 6 oz / 1½ cups walnuts or
pecan nuts, chopped

Serves 10

1

In a mixing bowl, combine the caster sugar, oil, eggs and carrots. Beat for 2 minutes.

2

Sift the dry ingredients into another bowl. Add in batches to the carrot mixture, mixing well after each addition. Preheat the oven to 190°C / 375°F / Gas Mark 5. Grease and flour two 23 cm / 9 in round layer cake tins.

3

Divide the cake mixture evenly between the prepared cake tins. Bake for 35–45 minutes, or until a skewer inserted in the centre of a cake comes out clean. Cool in the tins for 10 minutes, then transfer the cakes to wire racks to cool completely.

4

Beat all the icing ingredients except the nuts in a bowl until smooth. Sandwich the layers together with one-third of the icing, then spread the remaining icing over the top and sides of the cake, swirling it to make a decorative finish. Sprinkle the nuts around the rim.

Maple Walnut Pie

This pie is deliciously naughty – but nice.

INGREDIENTS

*3 eggs
salt
50 g / 2 oz / ¼ cup granulated sugar
50 g / 2 oz / ¼ cup butter, melted
250 ml / 8 fl oz / 1 cup pure maple
syrup
115 g / 4 oz / 1 cup walnuts, chopped
whipped cream, to decorate*

For the pastry
*50 g / 2 oz / ½ cup plain flour
50 g / 2 oz / ½ cup wholemeal flour
50 g / 2 oz / ¼ cup butter, diced
40 g / 1½ oz / 3 tbsp hard white
vegetable fat, diced
1 egg yolk
30–45 ml / 2–3 tbsp iced water*

Serves 8

1

For the pastry, mix the flours and a pinch of salt in a bowl. Rub in the fats until the mixture resembles breadcrumbs. Stir in the egg yolk and just enough water to bind the dough. Gather it into a ball, wrap in greaseproof paper and chill for 20 minutes.

2

Preheat the oven to 220°C / 425°F / Gas Mark 7. On a lightly floured surface, roll out the dough and line a 23 cm / 9 in flan tin. Trim the edge. To decorate, roll out the trimmings and stamp out small heart shapes. Brush the edge of the pastry case with water, then arrange the dough hearts around the rim.

3

Prick the bottom of the pastry case with a fork. Line with crumpled foil and bake for 10 minutes. Remove the foil and bake for 3–6 minutes more until golden brown.

4

In a bowl, whisk the eggs, a pinch of salt and the sugar together. Stir in the melted butter and maple syrup. Put the pastry case on a baking sheet. Pour in the filling, then sprinkle the nuts over the top. Bake for 35 minutes or until just set. Cool on a rack. Decorate with whipped cream.

Lemon Meringue Pie

This tasty pie would make a perfect end to a simple summer picnic. Served cold,
it needs no accompaniment.

grated rind and juice of 1 large lemon
250 ml / 8 fl oz / 1 cup water
25 g / 1 oz / 2 tbsp butter
200 g / 7 oz / scant 1 cup sugar
45 ml / 3 tbsp cornflour mixed to a
paste with 15 ml / 1 tbsp water
3 eggs, separated
pinch each of salt and cream of tartar

For the pastry
115 g / 4 oz / 1 cup plain flour
½ tsp salt
75 g / 3 oz / 6 tbsp hard white
vegetable fat, diced
30 ml / 2 tbsp iced water

Serves 8

NOTE
For Lime Meringue Pie, substitute the
grated rind and juice of 2 medium-size
limes for the lemon.

1

For the pastry, sift the flour and salt into a
bowl. Rub in the fat until the mixture
resembles breadcrumbs. Stir in just enough
water to bind the dough and roll out.

2

Line a 23 cm / 9 in flan tin with the pastry,
allowing the pastry to overhang the edge
by 1 cm / ½ in. Fold the overhang under
and crimp the edges. Chill the pastry case
for at least 20 minutes. Preheat the oven to
200°C / 400°F / Gas Mark 6.

3

Prick the pastry all over with a fork. Line
with crumpled foil and bake for
12 minutes. Remove the foil and bake for
6–8 minutes more, until golden.

4

In a saucepan, combine the lemon rind and
juice with the water. Add the butter and
115g / 4 oz / ½ cup of the sugar. Bring the
mixture to the boil. Mix the cornflour paste
with the egg yolks. Add to the lemon
mixture and return to the boil, whisking
continuously for about 5 minutes until the
mixture thickens. Cover the surface with
damp, greaseproof paper to prevent a skin
from forming. Leave to cool.

5

For the meringue, beat the egg whites with the salt and cream of tartar until they hold stiff peaks. Add the remaining sugar and beat until glossy.

6

Spoon the lemon mixture into the pastry case and spread level. Spoon the meringue on top, smoothing it up to the edge of the pastry to seal. Bake for 12–15 minutes, or until the meringue is tinged with gold.

The Farmhouse Pantry

Walk into the farmhouse pantry and discover a
wonderful array of pickles, chutneys, jams and jellies.
There are flavoured oils, too, and cheeses packed in
olive oil to be given as gifts or saved for special
occasions. The colours are glorious, the contents superb.
The following section provides recipes that will allow
you to enjoy the fruits of your labour all year round.

Tomato Chutney

*This spicy chutney is delicious with a selection of cheeses and biscuits,
or with cold meats.*

INGREDIENTS

INGREDIENTS

900 g / 2 lb tomatoes, skinned   225 g / 8 oz / 1⅛ cups caster sugar
225 g / 8 oz / 1⅓ cups raisins   600 ml / 1 pint / 2½ cups
225 g / 8 oz onions, chopped   malt vinegar

Makes 4 × 450 g / 1 lb jars

1

Chop the tomatoes roughly. Put them in
a preserving pan.

2

Add the raisins, onions and caster sugar.

3

Pour over the vinegar. Bring to the boil
and let it simmer for 2 hours, uncovered.
Pot into sterilized jars. Seal with a waxed disc
and cover with a tightly fitting cellophane
top. Store in a cool, dark place. The chutney
will keep unopened for up to a year. Once
opened, store in the fridge and consume
within a week.

Green Apple Chutney

This family recipe is wonderful with grilled sausages and baked ham.

INGREDIENTS

1 kg / 2¼ lb green apples
3–4 garlic cloves
1 litre / 1¾ pints / 4 cups malt vinegar
450 g / 1 lb / 2⅔ cups dates, chopped
115 g / 4 oz / ⅔ cup preserved stem
ginger, chopped
450 g / 1 lb / 2⅔ cups seedless raisins
450 g / 1 lb / 2⅔ cups soft brown
sugar
½ tsp cayenne pepper
30 ml / 2 tbsp salt

Makes about 2.75 kg / 6 lb

1

Cut the unpeeled apples into quarters,
remove the cores and chop coarsely. Peel
and chop the garlic and place it in a
saucepan with the apple.

2

Pour over the vinegar and boil until the
apples are soft. Add all the other
ingredients. Boil gently for 45 minutes.
Spoon the mixture into warm, sterilized
jars. Seal with a waxed disc and cover with
a tightly fitting cellophane top.

Green Tomato Chutney

*Unripened tomatoes are a culinary success rather than a horticultural failure when
transformed into a delicious chutney.*

INGREDIENTS

2 onions, chopped
1 kg / 2¼ lb green tomatoes, quartered
450 g / 1 lb apples, cored and
chopped, but not peeled
1 litre / 1¾ pints / 4 cups malt vinegar
425 g / 15 oz / 2½ cups soft
brown sugar
250 g / 9 oz / 1½ cups sultanas
7.5 ml / 1½ tsp mustard powder
5 ml / 1 tsp ground cinnamon
¼ tsp ground cloves
¼ tsp cayenne pepper

Makes about 2.5 kg / 5½ lb

1

Place the chopped onions in a large
preserving pan. Add the tomatoes and
apples. Stir in all the remaining ingredients
and heat gently, stirring until the sugar has
dissolved.

2

Bring to the boil, then simmer uncovered,
stirring occasionally, for 1½ hours. Pour
into warm, sterilized jars. Seal with a
waxed disc and cover with a cellophane top.

OPPOSITE (FROM LEFT):
Green Tomato Chutney,
Green Apple Chutney,
Windfall Pear Chutney.

222

Windfall Pear Chutney

The apparently unusable bullet-hard pears that litter the ground underneath
old pear trees after high winds are ideal for this tasty chutney.

INGREDIENTS

675 g / 1½ lb pears, peeled and cored
3 onions, chopped
175 g / 6 oz / 1 cup raisins
1 cooking apple, cored and chopped
50 g / 2 oz / ⅓ cup preserved stem ginger
115 g / 4 oz / 1 cup walnuts, chopped
1 garlic clove, chopped
grated rind and juice of 1 lemon
600 ml / 1 pint / 2½ cups cider vinegar
175 g / 6 oz / 1 cup soft brown sugar
2 cloves
5 ml / 1 tsp salt

Makes about 2 kg / 4½ lb

1

Chop the pears roughly and put them in a bowl. Add the onions, raisins, apple, ginger, walnuts and garlic, with the lemon juice and rind. Put the vinegar, sugar, cloves and salt into a saucepan. Gently heat, stirring until the sugar has dissolved, then bring to the boil briefly and pour over the fruit. Cover and leave overnight.

2

Tip the mixture into a preserving pan and boil gently for 1½ hours until soft. Spoon into warm, sterilized jars. Seal with a waxed disc and cover with a cellophane top.

Tarragon and Champagne Mustard

This delicate mustard is very good with cold seafood.

INGREDIENTS

30 ml / 2 tbsp mustard seeds
75 ml / 5 tbsp champagne vinegar
115 g / 4 oz / 1 cup mustard powder
115 g / 4 oz / ²⁄₃ cup soft brown sugar
2.5 ml / ½ tsp salt
50 ml / 3½ tbsp virgin olive oil
60 ml / 4 tbsp fresh tarragon, chopped

Makes about 250 g / 9 oz

1

Soak the mustard seeds overnight in the vinegar. Pour the mixture into a blender, add the mustard powder, sugar and salt and blend until smooth. With the motor running, gradually add the oil through the hole in the lid. Stir in the tarragon. Pour the mustard into sterilized jars, seal and store in a cool place.

Honey Mustard

Honey mustard is richly flavoured and is delicious in sauces and salad dressings.

INGREDIENTS

225 g / 8 oz / 1½ cups mustard seeds
15 ml / 1 tbsp ground cinnamon
½ tsp ground ginger
300 ml / ½ pint / 1¼ cups white wine vinegar
90 ml / 6 tbsp dark runny honey

Makes about 500 g / 1¼ lb

1

Mix the mustard seeds and spices in a bowl, pour on the vinegar and leave to soak overnight. Place the mixture in a mortar and pound to a paste. Gradually work in the honey. The finished mustard should resemble a stiff paste, so add extra vinegar if necessary. Store the mustard in sterilized jars in the fridge. Use within 4 weeks.

Horseradish Mustard

Horseradish mustard is a tangy relish that is an excellent accompaniment to cold meats, smoked fish or cheese.

INGREDIENTS

45 ml / 3 tbsp mustard seeds
250 ml / 8 fl oz / 1 cup boiling water
115 g / 4 oz / 1 cup mustard powder
115 g / 4 oz / ½ cup granulated sugar
120 ml / 4 fl oz / ½ cup white wine or cider vinegar
60 ml / 4 tbsp olive oil
5 ml / 1 tsp lemon juice
30 ml / 2 tbsp horseradish sauce

Makes about 400 g / 14 oz

1

Place the mustard seeds in a heatproof bowl, pour the boiling water over and leave for 1 hour. Drain, then tip into a blender. Add the remaining ingredients and blend the mixture to a smooth paste. Spoon it into sterilized jars. Store in the fridge and use within 3 months.

OPPOSITE (FROM LEFT): Honey Mustard, Horseradish Mustard, Tarragon and Champagne Mustard.

Mint Sauce

Mint sauce is the classic accompaniment to roast lamb.

INGREDIENTS

1 large bunch mint
105 ml / 7 tbsp boiling water
150 ml / ¼ pint / ⅔ cup wine vinegar
30 ml / 2 tbsp granulated sugar

Makes 250 ml / 8 fl oz / 1 cup

1

Chop the mint finely and place it in a 600 ml / 1 pint / 2½ cup jug. Pour on the boiling water and leave to infuse. When lukewarm, add the vinegar and sugar. Pour into a clean bottle and store in the fridge.

Tomato Ketchup

The true tomato taste shines through in this homemade sauce.

INGREDIENTS

2.25 kg / 5–5¼ lb very ripe tomatoes
1 onion
6 cloves
4 allspice berries
6 black peppercorns
1 fresh rosemary sprig
25 g / 1 oz fresh root ginger, sliced
1 celery heart, chopped
30 ml / 2 tbsp soft brown sugar
60 ml / 4 tbsp raspberry vinegar
3 garlic cloves, peeled
15 ml / 1 tbsp salt

Makes 2.75 kg / 6 lb

1

Skin and seed the tomatoes, then chop them finely and place in a large saucepan. Stud the onion with the cloves, tie it with the allspice, peppercorns, rosemary and ginger in a double layer of muslin and add to the saucepan. Stir in the celery, sugar, vinegar, garlic and salt.

2

Bring the mixture to the boil over a high heat, stirring occasionally. Reduce the heat and simmer for 1½–2 hours, stirring frequently until reduced by half. Purée the mixture in a blender or food processor, then return to the pan and bring to the boil. Reduce the heat and simmer for 15 minutes, then bottle in clean, sterilized jars. Store in the fridge. Use within 2 weeks.

Traditional Horseradish Sauce

Fresh horseradish root is extremely potent, but its effects can be alleviated if it is scrubbed and peeled underwater and a food processor is used to do the fine chopping or grating.

INGREDIENTS

45 ml / 3 tbsp horseradish root, freshly grated
15 ml / 1 tbsp white wine vinegar
5 ml / 1 tsp caster sugar
pinch of salt
150 ml / ¼ pint / ⅔ cup thick double cream, for serving

Makes about 175 ml / 6 fl oz / ¾ cup

1

Place the grated horseradish in a bowl. Stir in the vinegar, sugar and a pinch of salt.

2

Pour the sauce into a sterilized jar. It can be kept for up to 6 months in the fridge. A couple of hours before you intend to serve it, stir in the cream.

OPPOSITE: *Each of these sauces is a powerful reduction of its main ingredients.*

Mushrooms Preserved in Oil

The method of preserving in oil is ideally suited to good quality, firm mushrooms. The oil takes on a delicious mushroom flavour, and can be used to make special salad dressings.

INGREDIENTS

250 ml / 8 fl oz / 1 cup white wine vinegar
150 ml / ¼ pint / ⅔ cup water
5 ml / 1 tsp salt
1 fresh thyme sprig
½ bay leaf
1 fresh red chilli (optional)
450 g / 1 lb assorted wild mushrooms
400 ml / 14 fl oz / 1⅔ cups virgin olive oil

Makes 500 ml / 18 fl oz / 2 cups

1

Bring the vinegar and water to a simmer in a stainless steel pan. Add the salt, thyme, bay leaf and chilli (if using). Infuse for 15 minutes. Add the mushrooms.

2

Simmer for 10 minutes. Drain the mushrooms thoroughly, then spoon them into a sterilized preserving jar.

3

Cover the mushrooms with oil, close the lid and label. Mushrooms in oil will keep in a cool place for up to 12 months.

Spiced Mushrooms in Alcohol

Mushrooms combine with caraway seeds, lemon and chilli to make this unusual aperitif.

INGREDIENTS

75 g / 3 oz winter chanterelle and oyster mushrooms
5 ml / 1 tsp caraway seeds
1 lemon
1 fresh red chilli
350 ml / 12 fl oz / 1½ cups vodka

Makes 350 ml / 12 fl oz / 1½ cups

1

Place the mushrooms, caraway seeds, lemon and whole chilli in a clean preserving jar or bottle.

2

Pour in the vodka and leave for 2–3 weeks until the mushrooms no longer float. Chill thoroughly before straining and serving.

Pickled Mushrooms

Pickled mushrooms not only look good on the pantry shelf, they also taste delicious, especially when dressed with a little olive oil. In this recipe shiitake mushrooms take on an oriental flavour, although other firm mushrooms and spices can be used.

INGREDIENTS

250 ml / 8 fl oz / 1 cup white wine vinegar
150 ml / ¼ pint / ⅔ cup water
5 ml / 1 tsp salt
1 fresh red chilli
10 ml / 2 tsp coriander seeds
10 ml / 2 tsp szechuan pepper or anise-pepper
250 g / 9 oz shiitake mushrooms, halved if large

Makes 500 ml / 18 fl oz / 2 cups

1

Bring the wine vinegar and water to a simmer in a stainless steel pan. Add the salt, whole chilli, coriander seeds, szechuan pepper or anise-pepper and mushrooms and cook for 10 minutes.

2

Spoon the mushrooms and liquid into a sterilized 500 ml / 18 fl oz / 2¼ cup preserving jar. Seal, label and leave for at least 10 days before trying.

Chanterelle Vodka

For an unusual aperitif, try steeping chanterelle mushrooms in vodka. Chill well before straining and serving.

INGREDIENTS

350 ml / 12 fl oz / 1½ cups vodka
75 g / 3 oz young chanterelle mushrooms, trimmed

Makes 350 ml / 12 fl oz / 1½ cups

1

Place the chanterelle mushrooms in a clean preserving bottle or jar.

2

Pour in the vodka, cover and leave at room temperature. Chanterelle vodka is ready when the mushrooms have dropped to the bottom.

Piccalilli

The piquancy of this relish partners well with sausages, bacon or ham.

<u>INGREDIENTS</u>

675 g / 1½ lb cauliflower   5 ml / 1 tsp dry mustard powder
450 g / 1 lb small onions   10 ml / 2 tsp cornflour
350 g / 12 oz French beans   600 ml / 1 pint / 2½ cups vinegar
5 ml / 1 tsp ground turmeric

Makes 3 × 450 g / 1 lb jars

1

Cut the cauliflower into tiny florets.

2

Peel the onions and top and tail
the French beans.

3

In a small saucepan, measure in the turmeric,
mustard powder and cornflour, and pour
over the vinegar. Stir well and simmer
for 10 minutes.

4

Pour the vinegar mixture over the vegetables
in a pan, mix well and simmer
for 45 minutes.

5

Pour into sterilized jars. Seal each jar with a
waxed disc and a tightly fitting cellophane
top. Store in a cool dark place. The piccalilli
will keep unopened for up to a year. Once
opened store in the fridge and consume
within a week.

Dill Pickle

Dill is easy to grow and is a delightful herb. It goes well with fish and gives a superb flavour to this popular pickle.

INGREDIENTS

6 small cucumbers
475 ml / 16 fl oz / 2 cups water
1 litre / 1¾ pints / 4 cups white wine vinegar
115 g / 4 oz / ½ cup salt
3 bay leaves
45 ml / 3 tbsp dill seed
2 garlic cloves, slivered

Makes about 2.5 litres / 4 pints / 10 cups

1

Slice the cucumbers into medium-thick slices. Put the water, vinegar and salt in a saucepan. Bring to the boil, then immediately remove from the heat.

2

Layer the herbs and garlic between slices of cucumber in sterilized preserving jars until the jars are full, then cover with the warm salt and vinegar mixture. When the liquid is cold, close the jars. Leave on a sunny windowsill for at least 1 week before using.

Rhubarb and Ginger Mint Jam

Ginger mint is easily grown in the garden, and is just the thing to boost the flavour of rhubarb jam.

2 kg / 4½ lb rhubarb
250 ml / 8 fl oz / 1 cup water
juice of 1 lemon
5 cm / 2 in piece of fresh root ginger,
1.4 kg / 3 lb / 6 cups granulated sugar
115 g / 4 oz / ⅔ cup preserved stem ginger, chopped
30–45 ml / 2–3 tbsp fresh ginger mint leaves, very finely chopped

Makes about 2.75 kg / 6 lb

NOTE
To confirm the setting point, spoon a little of the jam on to a cold saucer. Leave for 2 minutes. A skin should have formed on the jam which will wrinkle if you push it gently with your finger.

1

Cut the rhubarb into short lengths. Place the rhubarb, water and lemon juice in a preserving pan and bring to the boil. Peel and bruise the root ginger and add to the pan. Reduce the heat and simmer, stirring frequently, until the rhubarb is soft.

2

Remove the ginger. Add the sugar and stir until dissolved. Boil rapidly for 10–15 minutes, or until setting point is reached. Skim off scum from the surface of the jam, then add the stem ginger and the chopped ginger mint leaves. Pour into sterilized glass jars, seal with waxed paper discs and cover with tightly fitting cellophane tops.

Apple and Mint Jelly

This jelly is delicious served with garden peas, as well as the more traditional rich roasted meat such as lamb.

INGREDIENTS

900 g / 2 lb Bramley cooking apples
granulated sugar
45 ml / 3 tbsp chopped fresh mint

Makes 3 × 450 g / 1 lb jars

1

Chop the apples roughly and put them in a preserving pan.

2

Add enough water to cover. Simmer until the fruit is soft.

3

Pour through a jelly bag, allowing it to drip overnight. Do not squeeze the bag or the jelly will become cloudy.

4

Measure the amount of juice. To every 600 ml / 1 pint / 2½ cups of juice, add 500 g / 1¼ lb / 2¾ cups granulated sugar.

5

Place the juice and sugar in a large pan and heat gently. Dissolve the sugar and then bring to the boil. Test for setting, by pouring about 15 ml / 1 tbsp into a saucer and leaving to cool slightly. If a wrinkle forms on the surface when pushed with a fingertip, the jelly will set. When a set is reached, leave to cool.

6

Stir in the mint and pot into sterilized jars. Seal each jar with a waxed disc and a tightly fitting cellophane top. Store in a cool, dark place. The jelly will keep unopened for up to a year. Once opened, keep in the fridge and consume within a week.

Rosemary-flavoured Oil

This pungent oil is ideal drizzled over meat or vegetables before grilling.

INGREDIENTS

600 ml / 1 pint / 2½ cups olive oil
5 fresh rosemary sprigs

Makes 600 ml / 1 pint / 2½ cups

1

Heat the oil until warm but not too hot.

2

Add four rosemary sprigs and heat gently. Put the reserved rosemary sprig in a clean bottle. Strain the oil, pour in the bottle and seal tightly. Allow to cool and store in a cool, dark place. Use within a week.

Thyme-flavoured Vinegar

This vinegar is delicious sprinkled over salmon intended for poaching.

INGREDIENTS

600 ml / 1 pint / 2½ cups
white-wine vinegar
5 fresh thyme sprigs
3 garlic cloves, peeled

Makes 600 ml / 1 pint / 2½ cups

1

Warm the vinegar.

2

Add four thyme sprigs and the garlic and heat gently. Put the reserved thyme sprig in a clean bottle, strain the vinegar, and add to the bottle. Seal tightly, allow to cool and store in a cool, dark place. The vinegar may be kept unopened for up to 3 months.

Yogurt Cheese in Olive Oil

Simple cheesemaking has always been a farmhouse tradition.
This recipe comes from Greece and is based upon sheep's yogurt.

INGREDIENTS

800 g / 1¾ lb / 3½ cups Greek sheep's yogurt
2.5 ml / ½ tsp salt
10 ml / 2 tsp dried chillies, crushed, or chilli powder
15 ml / 1 tbsp fresh rosemary, chopped
15 ml / 1 tbsp fresh thyme or oregano, chopped
about 300 ml / ½ pint / 1¼ cups olive oil, preferably garlic-flavoured

Makes about 900 g / 2 lb

NOTE
If your kitchen is particularly warm, find a cooler place to suspend the cheese. Alternatively, drain the cheese in the fridge, suspending the bag from one of the shelves.

1

Sterilize a 30 cm / 12 in square of muslin by steeping it in boiling water. Drain and lay over a large plate. Mix the yogurt with the salt and tip on to the centre of the muslin. Bring up the sides of the muslin and tie firmly with string.

2

Suspend the bag from a kitchen cupboard handle or similar suitable hook, allowing a bowl to be placed underneath to catch the whey. Leave for 2–3 days until the yogurt stops dripping.

3

Mix the chillies and herbs together. Take teaspoonfuls of the cheese and roll into balls with your hands. Carefully lower into two sterilized 450 g / 1 lb glass preserving jars, sprinkling each layer with some of the herb mixture.

4

Pour the oil over the cheese until completely covered. Store in the fridge for up to 3 weeks. To serve the cheese, spoon out of the jars with a little of the flavoured olive oil and spread on slices of lightly toasted bread.

Bottled Cherry Tomatoes

Cherry tomatoes bottled in their own juices are the perfect accompaniment to country ham.

INGREDIENTS

1 kg / 2¼ lb cherry tomatoes
salt (see method)
granulated sugar (see method)
fresh basil leaves

5 garlic cloves per jar

Makes 1 kg / 2¼ lb

1

Preheat the oven to 120°C / 250°F / Gas Mark ½. Prick each tomato with a toothpick.

2

Pack the tomatoes into clean, dry 1 litre / 1¾ pint / 4 cup preserving jars, adding 5 ml / 1 tsp each of salt and sugar to each jar.

3

Fill the jars to within 2 cm / ¾ in of the top, tucking the basil leaves and garlic among the tomatoes. Rest the lids on the jars, but do not seal. Stand on a baking sheet lined with a layer of cardboard or newspaper and place in the oven. After about 45 minutes, when the juice is simmering, remove from the oven and seal. Store in a cool place and use within 6 months.

Pickled Beetroot

The rich colour and intense flavour of pickled beetroot makes it a perennial favourite.

INGREDIENTS

450 g / 1 lb beetroot, cooked and peeled
1 large onion, sliced
300 ml / ½ pint / 1¼ cups cider vinegar
150 ml / ¼ pint / ⅔ cup water
50 g / 2 oz / ¼ cup granulated sugar

Makes 450 g / 1 lb

1

Slice the beetroot and pack it into a jar, layering it with the sliced onion. Pour the vinegar and water into a saucepan. Add the sugar and bring to the boil.

2

Pour the liquid over the beetroot and seal the jar. Store in a cool place and use within 1 month, or longer if kept in the fridge.

VARIATION

Red cabbage is easy to pickle by boiling in vinegar with sugar and spices.

Lemon and Lime Curd

Serve this creamy, tangy spread with toast or muffins,
instead of jam, for a delightful change.

INGREDIENTS

115 g / 4 oz / ½ cup unsalted butter	grated rind and juice of 2 lemons
	grated rind and juice of 2 limes
3 eggs	225 g / 8 oz / 1⅛ cups caster sugar

Makes 2 × 450 g / 1 lb jars

1

Set a heatproof mixing bowl over a large pan
of simmering water. Add the butter.

2

Lightly beat the eggs and add them
to the butter.

3

Add the lemon and lime rinds and juices,
then add the sugar.

4

Stir the mixture constantly until it thickens.
Pour into sterilized jars. Seal each jar with a
waxed disc and a tightly fitting cellophane top.
Store in a cool, dark place. The curd will
keep unopened for up to a month.
Once opened, keep in the fridge and
consume within a week.

Strawberry Jam

This classic recipe is always popular. Make sure the jam is allowed to cool before pouring into jars so the fruit doesn't float to the top.

INGREDIENTS

*1.5 kg / 3–3½ lb strawberries
juice of ½ lemon
1.5 kg / 3–3½ lb granulated sugar*

Makes about 2.25 kg / 5 lb

1

Hull the strawberries.

2

Put the strawberries in a pan with the lemon juice. Mash a few of the strawberries. Let the fruit simmer for 20 minutes or until softened.

3

Add the sugar and let it dissolve slowly over a gentle heat. Then let the jam boil rapidly until a setting point is reached.

4

Leave to stand until the strawberries are well distributed through the jam. Pot into sterilized jars. Seal each jar with a waxed disc and cover with a tightly fitting cellophane top. Store in a cool dark place. The jam may be kept unopened for up to a year. Once opened, keep in the fridge and consume within a week.

Crab Apple Jelly

Crab apple trees are so pretty with abundant flowers and glowing red fruit, and though their role in the garden is mainly decorative, this jelly is a delicious way to make use of the fruit.

INGREDIENTS

preserving sugar (see method)
1 kg / 2¼ lb crab apples
3 cloves
water (see method)

Makes about 1 kg / 2¼ lb from each 600 ml / 1 pint / 2½ cups liquid

1

Preheat the oven to 120°C / 250°F / Gas Mark ½. Put the preserving sugar in a heatproof bowl and warm in the oven for 15 minutes. Wash the apples and cut them in half but do not peel or core. Place the apples and cloves in a large saucepan.

2

Pour in water to cover. Bring to the boil, reduce the heat and simmer until soft. Strain the mixture into a bowl. Measure the juice and add 450 g / 1 lb / 2 cups sugar for each 600 ml / 1 pint / 2½ cups of juice. Pour into a pan and heat gently. Stir until the sugar dissolves, then boil rapidly until the setting point is reached. Pour into warm, sterilized jars and seal.

Rosehip and Apple Jelly

This recipe uses windfall apples and rosehips gathered from the hedgerows. The jelly is rich in vitamin C as well as full of flavour.

INGREDIENTS

1 kg / 2¼ lb windfall apples, peeled, trimmed and quartered
450 g / 1 lb firm, ripe rosehips
300 ml / ½ pint / 1¼ cups boiling water
preserving sugar (see method)

Makes about 1 kg / 2¼ lb from each 600 ml / 1 pint / 2½ cups liquid

OPPOSITE: Fruit jellies allow you to savour the taste of summer even during the winte months.

1

Place the quartered apples in a preserving pan with just enough water to cover them. Bring to the boil and cook until the apples are pulpy. Meanwhile, chop the rosehips coarsely in a food processor. Add the rosehips to the cooked apples with the boiling water. Leave to simmer for 10 minutes, then remove from the heat and allow to stand for 10 minutes more. Pour the mixture into a thick jelly bag suspended over a bowl and leave to strain overnight.

2

Preheat the oven to 120°C / 250°F / Gas Mark ½. Measure the juice and allow 400 g / 14 oz / 1¾ cups preserving sugar for each 600 ml / 1 pint / 2½ cups of liquid. Warm the sugar in the oven. Pour the juice into a pan and bring to the boil, stir in the warmed sugar until it has dissolved completely, then leave to boil until a setting point is reached. Finally, pour the jelly into warm, sterilized jars and seal securely.

Three-fruit Marmalade

*Home-made marmalade may be time-consuming but the results are
incomparably better than store-bought varieties.*

INGREDIENTS

350 g / 12 oz oranges
350 g / 12 oz lemons
700 g / 1½ lb grapefruit
*2.5 litres / 4½ pints / 10¼ cups
water*
2.75 kg / 6 lb granulated sugar

Makes 6 × 450 g / 1 lb jars

1

Rinse and dry the fruit.

2

Put the fruit in a preserving pan. Add the
water and let it simmer for about 2 hours.

3

Quarter the fruit, remove the pulp and
add it to the pan with the cooking liquid.

4

Cut the rinds into slivers, and add to the pan.
Add the sugar. Gently heat until the sugar
has dissolved. Bring to the boil and cook
until a setting point is reached. Leave to
stand for 1 hour to allow the peel to settle.
Pour into sterilized jars. Seal each jar with
a waxed disc and a tightly fitting cellophane
top. Store in a cool, dark place.

Poached Spiced Plums in Brandy

Bottling spiced fruit is a great way to preserve summer flavours for eating in winter. Serve these with whipped cream as a dessert.

INGREDIENTS

*600 ml / 1 pint / 2½ cups brandy
rind of 1 lemon, peeled in a
long strip
350 g / 12 oz / 1⅔ cups
caster sugar
1 cinnamon stick
900 g / 2 lb fresh plums*

Makes 900 g / 2 lb

1

Put the brandy, lemon rind, sugar and cinnamon stick in a large pan and heat gently to dissolve the sugar. Add the plums and poach for 15 minutes, or until soft. Remove with a slotted spoon.

2

Reduce the syrup by a third by rapid boiling. Strain it over the plums. Bottle the plums in large sterilized jars. Seal tightly and store for up to 6 months in a cool, dark place.

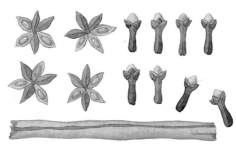

Spiced Pickled Pears

*These delicious pears are the perfect accompaniment for cooked ham
or cold meat salads.*

INGREDIENTS

900 g / 2 lb pears
600 ml / 1 pint / 2½ cups
white-wine vinegar
225 g / 8 oz / 1⅛ cups caster sugar
1 cinnamon stick
5 star anise
10 whole cloves

Makes 900 g / 2 lb

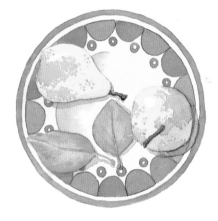

1

Peel the pears, keeping them whole
and leaving on the stalks. Heat the vinegar
and sugar together until the sugar has melted.
Pour over the pears and poach for 15 minutes.

2

Add the cinnamon, star anise and cloves
and simmer for 10 minutes. Remove the
pears and pack tightly into sterilized jars.
Simmer the syrup for a further 15 minutes
and pour it over the pears. Seal the jars
tightly and store in a cool, dark place. The
pears will keep for up to a year unopened.
Once opened, store in the fridge and
consume within a week.

Peach Wine

This delicious wine is intended to be made and drunk during the summer, either on its own or diluted with soda water.

INGREDIENTS

6 ripe peaches
1 litre / 1¾ pints / 4 cups dry white wine
200 g / 7 oz / scant 1 cup caster sugar
175 ml / 6 fl oz / ¾ cup eau de vie

Makes about 1.2 litres / 2 pints / 5 cups

1

Peel the peaches, cut them in half and remove the stones. Put them in a pan with the white wine and poach for about 15 minutes, until tender. Cover and allow to stand overnight.

2

Remove the peaches, then strain the liquid through a coffee filter. Add the sugar and eau de vie and stir to dissolve the sugar. Pour the liquid into clean, dry, sterilized bottles and cork. Store in the fridge. Drink within 2 weeks. Serve well chilled.

Mulberry Ratafia

A glut of mulberries provides a marvellous excuse for making this delicious drink.

INGREDIENTS

mulberries
caster sugar
vodka, brandy or gin

1

Fill clean, dry, sterilized jars with clean fruit. Pour in caster sugar so that it comes one-third of the way up the jar, then fill to the top with the spirit of your choice. Seal the jars and shake them to help the sugar dissolve. Store for at least 2 months.

2

Strain off the fruit (which you can use to make a delicious apple pie) and bottle the ratafia in clean, dry, sterilized bottles and seal securely. It should keep indefinitely if stored in airtight bottles.

Sloe Gin

This is a real country drink, traditionally used to celebrate high days and holidays. Sloes are gathered from the hedgerows after the first frosts, and the first bottle is ready for Christmas.

INGREDIENTS

sloes
caster sugar
gin

1

Wash the sloes and remove the stalks. Prick each sloe with a toothpick or needle, then pack the fruit into a wide-necked jar or bottle. Pour in caster sugar so that it comes halfway up the jar, then fill to the top with gin and seal.

2

Before drinking, strain off the sloes and decant into a clean bottle.

OPPOSITE (FROM LEFT): Mulberry Ratafia, Sloe Gin, Peach Wine.

Index

INDEX